When The World Was Whole

WHEN THE WORLD WAS WHOLE

Three Centuries of Memories

by
Charles Fenyvesi

PICADOR

published by Pan Books

First published in the United States of America by
Viking Penguin, New York, a division of Penguin Books USA Inc
This Picador edition published 1991 by Pan Books Ltd,
Cavaye Place, London SW10 9PG
1 3 5 7 9 8 6 4 2
© Charles Fenyvesi 1990
ISBN 0 330 31496 3

Photographs from the author's collection.
Frontispiece photograph: my grandparents
Roza and Karl Schwarcz

Printed and bound in Great Britain by Billing and Sons Ltd, Worcester

This book is dedicated to the hope that my children—Shamu, Daniel, and Malka—and their children will, too, recognize themselves in their ancestors.

Giving Thanks

The stories in this volume were gathered from many relatives, and they are the ones I owe the most. The list begins with a duo of Schwarcz storytellers no longer with us: Uncle Shumi, who assumed the role of the family historian in Budapest, and his cousin Shamu who spun out his versions while sitting in his tiny kitchen in Beersheba and saved the best portions for the times the two of us went out for a stroll. Often disagreeing with them on critical details has been my mother, Anna, who wrote her own heartfelt memoirs. Additional text and commentary were offered by my uncles Anti and Bédi, both now retired farmers in Israel under the name of Sade; and by cousins Ági Békés and Magda Erdös in Budapest, and Kató Schwarcz and Zvi (Pali) Sinai in Israel. Among my younger cousins, Levente Thury shored me up with his wisdom and unquestioning commitment; Andrea Szegö, Zhuzhi Grossman, and Tal Sade asked questions which helped me more than they know. They were all delighted to be engaged in the project and, regardless of their chronological ages, they all treated me with the species of tender sympathy that older people reserve for a young man in love.

I am grateful to my wife, Lizou, who first suggested that I write the book and whose humor and sarcasm pruned my sentimental excesses, and to our son Shamu who scrutinized the manuscript for colloquialisms and other lapses of an errant father.

Valuable words of advice and encouragement came from choice friends: Joel Garreau of *The Washington Post*, now working on his book on the new American city; Helen Epstein, author of *Children of the Holocaust*; Rabbi Eugene Lipman, author of several books on Judaica; Count Ferdinand von Trauttsmandorff of Vienna and a student of Middle European history. I also want to express my appreciation to the publications where some of the stories were first printed, albeit in a different form: *The Washington Post, Moment* magazine, *Rodale's Organic Gardening*, and *Washington Jewish Week*.

I am beholden to my friend and literary agent Joseph Spieler whose gentle prodding never tightened into a nudge and whose editing scalpel was most useful, and to my editor Dan Frank who inspired me by falling in love with the book when it consisted of only a few chapters and by persisting in his affections until it was completed.

Contents

Ready for a ride in 1905, in front of the Schwarcz house in the village of Gyulaj. Next to the driver is my uncle Shumi, six years old; in the back of the carriage between two adults, who are probably relatives, is Aunt Elza, seven. The little girl in the white dress and broad-brimmed hat perhaps is also a relative.

Prologue

E ver since I remember remembering, I have heard stories about my ancestors, whose lives pulsed with the
teachings of two rabbis who performed what people
called miracles: the Baal Shem Tov, who wandered through
the villages of the Carpathian mountains, and Isaac Taub,
who shepherded a congregation of about a hundred souls in
the little town of Kálló, on the northeastern edge of Hungary's
Great Plain. These two eighteenth century rabbis of blessed
memory broke rank with their colleagues when they declared
that misery and oppression are not inevitable, and that we
can and must improve the world; that while suspicion and
revenge unleash new cycles of hatred, it is always possible
to start anew; that the vast Gentile world which surrounds
the little Jewish world is not immutably and forever hostile,
and that Gentiles are our partners in improving the world. If
there is one phrase that can sum up the advice of the two
rabbis, it is this: Do not fear! Or, better yet: Keep the gates
of your heart open!

I was seven when the Nazi noose tightened around us in
Hungary, and every day I saw my mother wait anxiously for
the mailman to bring postcards from her husband and her

mother, her brothers and sisters and cousins, who were being taken to concentration camps or forced-labor battalions. For me, a bedtime story about a forefather overcoming his fear of bandits and other evil spirits and living an unusually long life was more reassuring than all the wishful rumors about the Americans and the British being on their way to liberate us.

Our family stories had a cast of characters who were wholesome and as rooted in the land of Hungary as an old walnut tree. They suggested to me that the thugs I saw on the streets of Budapest marching off men, women, and children to be shot on the banks of the Danube river were not real people, but ghouls as insubstantial as those in a nightmare. I thought that the high-pitched, high-speed, hysterical voice on the radio—and even a child couldn't mistake Adolf Hitler's voice—simply had to run out of words, breath, and life. One day he would choke on the poison that he spewed out, I thought, and his followers would be swallowed up by an angry earth.

In my heart I was certain that one day my grandfather or great-grandfather would come on a horse-drawn wagon and take us all to a safe and beautiful place, which to me always meant the countryside. Having heard bedtime stories about my ancestors, I believed that both these men were still on this earth, but somewhere far away where only those gained entrance who were just and kind and generous. I believed they were watching what was happening to us, and that if ever our lives were in real danger, they would surely leave their hiding place to rescue their family at the last minute.

My parents and I were fortunate in evading the Nazis, but the larger part of our family did not survive.

Though I soon outgrew bedtime stories, I still wanted to

know more about my ancestors and I was annoyed that different relatives told different versions of the same story. Why couldn't my Uncle Shumi and his cousin Shamu, both born in the last year of the nineteenth century, agree on how their grandfather Samuel acquired his wealth—or how and why their generation lost it? Just exactly when and where did a carriage axle break on a critical journey through the snowdrifts of the Carpathian mountains?

"But what is the truth?" I kept asking. My relatives were apologetic. "This is how I heard it," each of them said, and would add, as the ultimate excuse: "All that happened long, long ago."

What upset Uncle Shumi, who eventually typed up a family history in response to my request, was that he had forgotten so much. "I can't tell you enough times how precious few of the stories I heard as a child I still remember," he wrote to me in 1966, in a Hungarian resonant with the cadences of the nineteenth century. "In my earlier years I did not delve into old documents and I neglected to listen to what old people from our village had to say. Now I am old and not very active. I am deeply sorry, and my conscience is wracked with guilt. It is nonetheless my duty to hand over to you the key to the nearly empty pantry of my memories."

I think it was soon after I became a father and had to tailor stories for my children's ages and interests that I began to appreciate why there are several versions to our family stories. Each variation is proof of the strength of the plot, I now know. An inventive adaptation is a storyteller's tribute to the story, and a thoughtful alteration is a sign of caring and appreciation.

In the stories I committed to writing in this volume, I have blended the different versions I heard, and I have tried to imagine what people of long ago might have said to each other. In one instance, I went as far as to attribute to a forefather a dream I had—because according to one account, he had had a dream projecting his good fortune. On a few occasions, I was buoyed by the strange and wonderful certainty that I got an event, a sequence, or a sentiment just right, and I felt like shouting: This is how it must have happened!

Such moments return me to my childhood, when I would fall asleep listening to a family story, and while on the edge of a dream, I could still hear a voice from the world which stayed awake, my mother's or grandmother's or uncle's, bringing the story to its conclusion. The horse-drawn wagon, laden with sheep's fleece or sacks of potatoes, rolled on, but I was by then snuggled next to the driver, my grandfather who hummed a melody, part Hebrew prayer and part Hungarian folk song, whose rhythm was set by the horse's cheerful trot. The dream, the story, the journey, were now mine.

When I woke I was no longer sure if the driver had been my grandfather, my great-grandfather, or perhaps someone more distant on a family tree that spans counties and continents and centuries. But I remembered the happiness while riding in the dream wagon.

After my uncle Shumi died, in 1988, I began thinking of putting together our family stories, many of which I had first heard from him. One night I dreamt I was driving a carlike vehicle that hovered over a hilly, verdant country road, when suddenly I saw Uncle Shumi coming from the other direction. He was out for a stroll, his pace brisk as in his younger days, and his arm around the shoulders of a child. I was the child.

I shouted to them and stepped on the brakes. "Speed up,"

said an American voice behind me, the stern voice of the bus driver who takes me to work in downtown Washington. "You are allowed to operate this time-machine on the condition that you keep a steady speed. You may not land. I repeat: You may not land!"

I stepped on the gas pedal, and they were gone in an instant.

A year later, during a visit to Hungary, I was listening to my cousin Andrea's wistful suggestion that those few of us who are left in the family ought to climb aboard a horse-drawn wagon, find our way back to Derzs, our ancestral village, and begin the family saga again. "But we no longer know how to cultivate land," another cousin, Levente, countered ruefully. "We no longer know those strategies that made our ancestors successful and wealthy and contented."

No one could disagree with Levente. But for the rest of the evening, all of us around the festive dinner table savored Andrea's idea of time travel.

Along with many of their fellow Jews, our forebears believed that the Baal Shem Tov, the gentle rabbi who was born in the Russian town of Okop around 1700, was joined in such harmony with heaven and earth that he could bring about miracles. At one time, for instance, the Baal Shem Tov petitioned God not to send the Angel of Death to fetch the soul of a mortally ill child. Indignant and angry, the rabbi reminded the Almighty that it is against the natural order for a child to die before his parents. God relented, and the child recovered and lived a long and healthy life.

When arguing against an edict of heaven or pleading a case of special favor for a deserving person, the Baal Shem

Tov retired to a forest. There he chanted a prayer appropriate to the occasion while standing under a densely branched walnut tree he had known from the time both he and the tree were young.

When confronted with a similar problem, the Baal Shem Tov's grandson, a famous rabbi in his own right, felt he did not need the walnut tree. Any tree would do, he decided, as long as he used the right prayer in the forest favored by the Baal Shem Tov.

The grandson's grandson, another renowned rabbi, moved too far from the forest to be able to visit it every time there was a need for special prayer. But he still knew the words, and he found that chanting the prayer was sufficient.

After two more generations, the words of the prayer were lost. But it is said that merely telling the story of how the Baal Shem Tov once brought about a miracle still has the power to alter the course of events.

In our days, with the passing of two more generations, we still have the story.

The will to remember is a force far stronger than a lapse of memory, and a mortal's greatest triumph is the one over time: digging up what was cast off and mending what was broken. Though the precise formula for performing magic may be lost, perhaps irretrievably, we should not cease asking for miracles.

We can still recapture bits and pieces from a world that was once whole, in which lives were aligned in secret symmetries, one good deed invoked another, and a gift from heaven passed from one generation to the next. Telling stories about such a world helps restore it, and the storyteller prescribes a miracle each time he recalls an instance of heaven bending to a human who pleads with a pure heart and a soul on fire. In my family tradition, we believe that such an appeal has the best chance of winning when it has the concurrence of the earth impatient for improvement and grateful for persistence.

A dream gives the first hint of a miracle, and Rabbi Isaac Taub, the Baal Shem Tov's Hungarian disciple, taught that we ought to pay attention to our dreams the way a traveller must pay attention to signs on the highway. Three generations before Sigmund Freud, Rabbi Taub untangled the dreams of people who went to him for advice and help. The rabbi searched for what the Talmud calls "big dreams" the way others look for buried treasures. In one instance, when arranging the marriage of an orphan entrusted to his care, Rabbi Taub found the right bride through his dreams and the boy's. And the rabbi interpreted—if not inspired—my family's founding dream of land and plenty.

"But is your story true?" my daughter, Malka, now ten, has been asking since she was six. "Tell me, Dad, did your grandparents really get married the way you say they got married? Are your stories about real people who actually lived?"

When they were little, my sons Shamu and Danny both wanted to know for sure whether our family really received a blessing from a rabbi who brought about miracles, and whether there really were such rabbis and miracles.

To all the questions, I say yes, firmly and unequivocally. These stories are by, of, and for our family. They are our truth. Ours to share.

When The World Was Whole

Cousin Yenö around the turn of the century. Owner of a pine
forest and a sawmill, he followed the family tradition of
launching a poor relative on what he called "the highway of
life" by presenting him with his first pair of walking shoes.

1.

In the Shadows of the Past

Heaven and earth conspire that everything which has been, be rooted and reduced to dust. Only the dreamers, who dream while awake, call back the shadows of the past and braid nets from unspun threads.
ISAAC BASHEVIS SINGER, *The Spinoza of Market Street*

In Belgrade's dingy railroad station, the time always seems to be half past midnight, and the trains are perpetually late. In the station's standing-room-only, cigarette-butt-littered tavern that never closes, an unshaven man in his midfifties sings one ditty after another in a throaty, hoarse baritone. His delivery suggests half entertainment, half prayer. Gripping a glass of wine, he addresses no one in particular. Most people pay no attention to him, but a few do listen, and one man even offers him money, which he declines with a wave of his bony hand.

One of his songs is about a Jewish virgin, the daughter of a rabbi who is arranging a marriage for her. Raven-haired and almond-eyed, she is as beautiful as he is wise, and no one from their hometown, a dusty overgrown village where two highways cross, is good enough for her, or for her father.

The song is in Serbo-Croatian, and the singer could be its author. Or, more likely, the song was passed down to him. Yugoslavia is in the Balkans, and the peninsula was Homer's wandering grounds, where the bardic tradition still lives.

It is possible that the singer has never knowingly met a rabbi's daughter, or a rabbi. It is also possible that he has

1

never knowingly spoken with a Jew. Bards are keepers of memories that are seldom their own. They may add to the oral treasury—and ambitious bards do—but the norm is to draw on what others have contributed. As it is with plum brandy, the older the song, the more it is cherished.

In East-Central Europe, a region buffeted between the immensities of Mother Russia and the refinements of Western civilization, Jews stood out for centuries as a separate tribe whose members were both mysterious and familiar, enviably rich and pitifully poor, vulnerable and powerful. In these closing years of the twentieth century, the authentic, distinct, historical Jew is turning into a folk memory: a fabled people joining, in the consciousness of the surviving nations, with the Habsburg bureaucrat, the Ottoman pasha, the Hun horseman, and the Roman legionnaire.

Government statistics still list tens of thousands of Jews in the region, nearly all living in the capitals. The vast majority are assimilated, hard to tell apart from their fellow citizens. Rabbis still lead services in improbably splendid synagogues, built a century ago in a now faraway age that harnessed sudden new wealth generated by capitalist expansion to the classic piety handed down from the Middle Ages. Under the red star of communism, now breaking apart, there has been neither wealth nor piety, yet Jews still gather for purposes other than paying vestigial tribute to their ancestors once a year, on the Day of Atonement. The most idealistic among them collect, as do Gentile friends who are hard put to explain their motives, fragments of a Jewish world that was once whole.

These days in Central Europe it is quaint and intriguing to be part-Jewish, and a distant rabbinical forefather, discovered after decades of amnesia, gussies up a family tree the way the whisper of an archduke's dalliance once did. "I believe my grandmother must have been Jewish," an otherwise cynical Yugoslav journalist born in the early years of the People's Republic confesses to me wistfully. With the cheerless grin of a survivor, he cites the Nazis' law of racial purity which doomed an Aryan whose genealogical documents revealed a single Jewish grandparent. While walking through Belgrade's old inner city, now in the throes of a rehabilitation project, he points to a hole, the size of a bomb crater, where workmen recently stumbled upon thick stone walls that he is convinced once belonged to a synagogue. He concedes that thus far archeologists don't have much evidence to support his thesis beyond the fact that they have found neither a cross nor a crescent in what was probably a public building. "Jews have lived between the Adriatic sea and the Drava river forever," he cries out, "and at least as far back as the Roman empire. And Jews build their synagogues to endure. 'Endure'—isn't that the password, isn't that the secret of the Jews?"

I am reminded of a legend that says that after an eleventh century Russian general destroyed the capital of the Khazars, a tribe living between the Black Sea and the Caspian Sea that had converted to Judaism, the shadows of the houses held their outlines for many years even though all the walls had been razed. The shadows held in the wind, it is claimed, as did their reflections in the water. I am also reminded of my godfather, Yenö, who sent me seven sturdy pairs of shoes, in progressively larger sizes, shortly before he was taken by the Nazis in 1944. Owner of a pine forest and a sawmill in the Carpathian mountains, near the source of the river Tisza, Yenö was a close relative. He was my father's cousin, and his wife was my mother's cousin, and he was delighted to have an opportunity to observe a shared family tradition: a

3

wealthy relative launches a poor one on "the highway of life" by providing his first pair of walking shoes.

We will never know if Yenö increased the number of shoes to seven pairs because he suspected that he would not live to buy any more presents, or because he believed that seven, a magic number, would multiply his godson's chances of survival. I was a teenager, soon to flee across the border to Austria and then off to the United States, and Yenö had long disappeared as a wisp of smoke over Auschwitz, when I grew out of the seventh pair of his shoes, which were a treasure in Hungary in the Stalinist poverty of the 1950s and fetched a good price after I was done with them. Every time I buy a pair of shoes I remember that out of Yenö's extended family of more than fifty people, only two survived the Nazis, and that no more than a handful of Jews are left in his town of Huszt, now part of the Soviet Union, and called Chust, where in his day more than twenty rabbis competed for the loyalties of five thousand Jews.

Nowhere along the Danube or its tributaries, the Drava and the Tisza, is there today a rabbi famous for his wisdom who attracts Jew and non-Jew looking to ease their troubled souls. The markets still smell of sausage and sheep cheese, apricots and dill and freshly baked bread, but there are no Jewish women shouting the praise of their wondrously fat geese, no Jewish bands playing at Jewish weddings, and no itinerant students of the Talmud eating at the table of a rich grain merchant or a poor but pious tailor. Jewish peddlers no longer wander from village to village, from county to county, selling ribbons and yarn and the latest cotton prints, and collecting from the peasants sacks of goosedown for filling comforters which are at the same time the warmest and the lightest, or pillows which prompt the sweetest of dreams; nor

4

do the peddlers buy up the plum harvest to distill kosher slivovitz, the best in the world. There are no more Jewish innkeepers and no more Jewish landowners.

No more, no more, no more.

In the eastern Hungarian town of Debrecen, where I was born, I meet with a thoughtful county official, a patriot with a mellifluous voice and an aching heart. To define himself in 1988, he cites nineteenth century Hungarian poetry: he is a sentinel on the frontier with Russia and Romania, and a caretaker of ruins left behind by four decades of the alien forces of communism. He hopes that by dint of hard work and under a new generation of leaders, his nation will recover its glory.

A descendant of Calvinist preachers, the county official represents the nationalist tradition of his community, the Protestant denomination which in the sixteenth and seventeenth centuries won over many Hungarians opposed to the Roman Catholic House of Habsburg. They constitute the majority in Debrecen, the city Hungarians call "the Calvinist Rome." It was in the austere Calvinist church that towers over Debrecen's main street and which is known simply as "the Big Temple" that the revolutionary parliament of 1849 voted to dethrone the Habsburgs, thus sealing Czar Nicholas I's decision to dispatch his armies to restore a fellow monarch overthrown by popular uprising.

The conversation goes on for hours and hours, and the county official's initial reserve, the armor of a Debrecen burgher, falls away layer by layer. Hungary has been a colony of the Russians, he says. While Russian jets land and take off from Debrecen's airport whenever they wish, a Hungarian plane needs a special permit. The Hungarian treasury has

supplied Soviet occupation forces with food and was required
to contribute to the upkeep of the Russians' far-flung empire
in Cuba, Vietnam, Ethiopia, and Afghanistan. At the same
time, the Kremlin did not allow itself a hint of sympathy for
the plight of the two-million-strong Hungarian minority in
Romania.

It is past midnight when he comes around to the subject
of what he calls "the dear old Jews." He laments their passing
the way Byron and Goethe lamented the vanishing of the
ancient Greeks or of the scribes who had illuminated man-
uscripts. "What secrets they must have known," he says with
a sigh, "we will never know. Those white-bearded old rabbis
knew everything. I mean everything!"

Born after the Second World War, he has no firsthand
knowledge of the twelve thousand Jews who once lived in his
town. He is aware that Jews, including descendants of Hungarian Jews, survive and prosper in other lands. But to his
way of thinking, Hungary is the fulcrum of the globe, and
the virtual disappearance of Jews from Debrecen, the country's second largest city with a population of two hundred
thousand, constitutes a loss to Hungary, rather than to the
Jewish people.

Hungary still boasts some hundred thousand Jews, 98 per-
cent of them living in Budapest, a metropolis of more than
two million. Nevertheless, the official in Debrecen asks, and
his questions are not just rhetorical: "Where are the real
Jews, the Jewish Jews? Aren't all our real Jews dead?"

I drive around in a rented car, looking up places I last saw
more than thirty years ago, when I was a student of literature
at the local university, named after Lajos Kossuth, leader of
the 1848 revolution, and took part, along with nearly all of

A descendant of Calvinist nobility and
an official in the Bureau of Birth Registry
in Debrecen, Erzsébet Dávid saved Jews
during the Nazi era by forging Christian
birth certificates for them.

The Schwarcz family in 1935 at the wedding of youngest
daughter Mara to Levente (center). My grandmother Róza is
seated to the left; her eldest daughter Elza to the right.
Standing, from left: Uncle Mishi, my mother Anna, Uncle
Anti (wearing glasses). On the far right is Uncle Shumi; next
to him is his wife Agnes.

my classmates, in the 1956 revolution. The university's marble facade is as solemnly symmetrical as the temple of Apollo after which it was modelled, and its spacious plaza is now crowded with couples holding hands and students with books under their arms. On November 4, 1956, the day the Kremlin dispatched its armies to crush the uprising, I was standing against the front wall, together with scores of my classmates, our hands above our heads. We were waiting for the Russian commander to shoot us, arrest us, or let us go. The last seemed the least likely.

Our ordeal had begun some time earlier in the morning when Russian tanks surrounded the university and someone with a loudspeaker announced that unless we laid down our rifles immediately, the tanks would open fire on us. Shortly before noon, another anonymous voice told us that we must all go home, and warned us not to show our faces anywhere near the university until "the appropriate authorities" gave us permission to return.

I drive by the hospital where I was born, in 1937, during the night of Debrecen's first air-raid exercise in preparation for the Second World War. A local newspaper published a light-hearted report about all that happened in town during the first blackout and duly noted the birth of two children. The other child, a girl, also was Jewish. Her life ended in an Auschwitz gas chamber, but her mother, sent to work in a munitions factory, survived.

After the war my mother and I ran into her on a street in Budapest. I cannot forget the look in her eyes which asked me, wordlessly: Why are you alive and why is my daughter dead?

In 1944 my father was in a forced-labor battalion, as were most able-bodied Hungarian Jewish males, but my mother and I were reasonably free to move about because we had acquired a new last name, Farkas, and the life-saving pieces of paper we had to carry with us at all times declared that my parents and I had been born Calvinists. The document was the same size as a page in the notebook I was supposed to fill, practicing the letters of the alphabet.

The forgery was by a close friend of my mother's, Erzsébet Dávid. For years she had been a frequent guest in my grand-mother Róza's house: a shy, frail lady with thick glasses and braids which she wore in a tight chignon. She had never married, and some family members suspected her of being in love with one or another of my uncles.

A descendant of Calvinist nobility from Transylvania, and the only child of a high court judge, Erzsébet Dávid was a devout Christian who was horrified by Nazi racism. As a high-ranking official in Debrecen's birth registry, she had access to blank forms and rubber stamps. She made out scores of Christian birth certificates for Jews, and she tried to persuade them to take the papers and leave for another town, preferably metropolitan Budapest, more than a hundred miles away, where it was harder for the authorities to check up on someone's identity than in Debrecen, a small town where people knew one another. But not everyone had the courage to go about with forged documents, nor was it clear to most Jews that being forced out of one's home and crowded into a newly created ghetto constituted the first step to a death camp in Hitler's Reich. Erzsébet Dávid suspected the worst and was astonished when most Jews refused to believe her.

The police caught a Jew claiming to be a Christian and identified his forged documents as coming from Erzsébet Dávid's office. She was arrested, and put on trial in the same courtroom once presided over by her father. The Hungarian prosecutor asked that her punishment be of "extreme severity" because she had stained her father's memory and betrayed "the sacred trust of the state" in falsifying documents.

The night before she was to be sentenced—and it was likely to be death—an American air raid destroyed much of the prison where she was held. She escaped unhurt, but in poor health made worse by her interrogation and imprisonment.

She was exonerated after the war and made director of the birth registry. She died in 1948, in the small room she rented not far from the Big Temple. Not a single relative accompanied her coffin to the cemetery, perhaps because she had none, or perhaps because none of them cared for her. She was buried by the Debrecen Jews whom she had helped during the war, and they raised a marble tombstone which declared her "the heroine of our times."

There aren't many people in Debrecen who remember her, and in the late 1980s neither my mother nor I could find her grave in the section where the cemetery records say she was buried.

It is a chilly, somber September afternoon, and an unsteady drizzle the color of lead fails to thicken into rain, but lends a dull sheen to the uneven expanse of gray cobblestones. Debrecen smells of wet wool and fried bacon.

I stop by one of the little taverns for which Debrecen is famous. Tavern keepers used to drop the names of the celebrated writers who had once been regular customers and who kept going back in the hope of unlocking the locals' stiff reserve. But today's employees, who work for the state, are in no mood to boast or even to make conversation. Their

10

customers take their eating and drinking seriously, and the portions are large. I drink espresso, a thick bitter brew. I listen. There is only occasional laughter, and words are sparse and carefully measured before and after they are uttered.

The townspeople are as I remember them: deliberate, dignified, distant. There are only two classes: an upper stratum combed, ironed, and starched as if ready for a photographer; and the rest, rumpled and disheveled, as if they slept in their clothes. Both look upon a stranger with wary eyes.

Except for the few heady days of the 1956 revolution, I don't remember feeling at home in the town of my birth. As a teenager, I used to wander through the side streets, lined with gaunt, assymetrical sycamores, in search of clues to what people didn't say. My favorite time for a walk was after nine in the evening, with most everyone asleep, which gave me a chance to imagine their dreams as I skipped over potholes. I could not believe that money was the only currency that mattered to them. I hoped to find passions masked by the banality, and intelligence hidden underneath the indifference. The only people I met were drunks thrown out of one tavern and on their way to another, eager to tell me in the meantime, as they leaned on my shoulders with both hands, that they loved or hated all Hungarians or Jews or Gypsies, or that they would always or never go back to their wives who were either saints or sluts.

In school I was taught that millions of years ago all of the Hungarian Great Plain, including its capital, Debrecen, had been covered by a sea that vanished in some global cataclysm. Perhaps Debrecen has not ceased to be a dried-out wilderness parched for rain and ideas, cheer and redemption. In the desert heat of the summer, the cloudless sky seems to choke the town; during the intense cold of winter, the burghers shut

11

themselves in their rooms to escape the bone-chilling winds.

Once again I walk up and down the narrow streets, turning this way and that. I can't find the dark, cavelike little synagogue that my maternal grandmother, Róza, used to attend and which reminded her of the synagogue in the village of Gyulaj where she had lived before the loss of the family estate and subsequent exile to Debrecen. She did not like the proud, imposing edifice of the town's main synagogue, which burned down, the cause of the fire never determined, shortly after the Second World War.

In the evening I learn that the little synagogue was recently razed, along with adjoining buildings, as part of an urban renewal project, and that the land on which it stood is now a municipal parking lot where I almost parked earlier in the day when I arrived. For some reason I didn't understand, I had driven out of the nearly empty expanse of asphalt. Disoriented, I was unable to find the hulking structure of the main hotel called Arany Bika, which translates as The Golden Bull. I ended up parking illegally on a street adjacent to the hotel.

I walk through the cramped, crooked back streets where poor Jews once lived in houses that huddled together like sheep in a thunderstorm. There is still one small synagogue, but a sign says it is open only on the Sabbath.

The street where my family once lived, named after the great nineteenth century reformer Count Széchenyi, is torn up, and passersby curse as they stumble over the cobblestones and dirt dumped on the pavement. The workers are surly. Standing in trenches they are supposed to dig six feet deep, they are replacing old sewers. The soil is sandy and porous, and a spade can handle most of the job, but the diggers keep having to use mattocks when they come upon hefty stones that spilled from walls raised centuries ago. The diggers curse the burghers who imported the stones from the Transylvanian mountains, curse the engineers who designed the sewers, and curse their own bad luck as laborers.

Debrecen is close to a thousand years old. From the beginning, it was a settlement of rich peasants and richer traders who erected high, thick walls of brick and stone around their properties. The gates were elaborate and massive, made of solid oak reinforced with straps and rivets of wrought iron. Living simply and trading cautiously, the burghers accumulated wealth in coins of gold and silver, which they hid in the hollow columns and false bottoms of meticulously crafted cupboards and armoires. Or they sealed in their treasures in the stone foundation walls of cavernous cellars, where they often took refuge because the town, a sprawling oasis in the center of a flat, treeless plain, had never raised a wall to hold off an armed force, but negotiated a ransom instead. Debrecen was, however, girdled by a deep ditch that prevented the wagons of traders from evading the gates and skipping payment of the high entrance fees that the town imposed on all outsiders for the privilege of buying and selling in its markets.

The burgher here called himself *civis*, using the proud Latin term for a citizen of Rome, the archetypal European city state, and he argued with king and nobleman to keep his rights as a free man of means. He was determined to shut out all not born within its confines. Until 1841, no Jew was allowed to spend a night within the city, let alone rent or buy a house.

I walk over to the house where my grandmother Róza lived before she was deported to Auschwitz in 1944. The gate, loose on its hinges, is ajar. The one-story building seems about to collapse. The mortar is turning into powder and drifts out from in between the bricks, and the red roof tiles are splitting. Built in the nineteenth century, the house was once a fine structure. It had dignity, so important to my gentrified forebears, but now it looks as if it had been part of an abjectly poor medieval ghetto.

I walk around the courtyard, once planted thick with shrubs and flowers, the work of my mother Anna, a born gardener. The brick-covered pathway used to be swept every morning, to help start the day with a clean slate. Now there are only a few neglected, unhappy plants, and the pathway is only partially visible underneath layers of mud, bottle caps, and cigarette butts.

Grandmother Róza's house in Debrecen today. Built in the nineteenth century, it was once a fine structure; now it looks as if it had been part of an abjectly poor medieval ghetto.

I search for the mezuzah—the finger-size talisman for protection that has a prayer encased in wood or metal—which Jews do not remove once they nail it to the doorpost and which Christians sometimes keep for good luck. But the doorframe is so riddled with nicks and nail holes that I can't even guess where the mezuzah might have been.

There is not a soul around, and I am thankful. For once I don't feel like having a conversation with locals, and I don't look for people who might have known my beloved, unforgettable grandmother. It is as if we had never lived in this town.

The next day, I drive across the Romanian border and enter the hilly, wooded land of Transylvania. The soil, stippled with rocks, is poor and best suited for herding sheep and for nourishing religious sects. For centuries, Transylvania appeared to be an extension of Byzantium, with people as stylized and hierarchical as if arrayed on an icon: the rich, clad in Italian velvet and Turkish silk, and the poor, dressed in coarse, homespun linens and wools, and each ethnic group wearing its own attire. Transylvania was once an independent principality balancing its antipathies for the sultan in Istanbul and for the emperor in Vienna, but is now a multi-ethnic province ruled from Bucharest to the south of the Carpathian mountains. When I visit, the tyrant Nicolae Ceausescu is still alive. He declared his reign to be the Golden Age, and he was determined to destroy structures of worship and habitation built before him.

Some thirty-five miles east of Debrecen, in the town Romanians call Oradea and Hungarians call Nagyvárad, a playwright who writes in Hungarian tells me he often visits the Jewish cemetery "for inspiration." He looks at the tombstones, reads the inscriptions if they are in Hungarian, and marvels at Hebrew letters, which he calls "rootlike" and which are incomprehensible to him. Many of the marble tombstones were intended as works of art, he says, while others just happen to be beautiful. In the stillness of the cemetery, the playwright hears voices. He is convinced that the Jewish dead are as talkative and argumentative as they were while alive, and all that a writer needs to do is "to listen and to listen deep."

He is a Calvinist married to a woman who comes from a family of ethnic Germans, yet another minority that migrated to Transylvania over the past millennium. His subject as a writer is life in Nagyvárad under Turkish occupation in the sixteenth and early seventeenth centuries, when the Ottoman sultan's power was at its height. Yet it is the Jewish cemetery, less than two hundred years old, which conveys to him "the torment of the past and a perpetual sense of loss." He says that the Jews have been swept out of the area, just like the Turks. He fears that the same will happen to his fellow Hungarians, whose ancestors included Hun horsemen who stayed behind after the retreat to Central Asia following Attila's death and who have become a persecuted minority during the past seven decades of Romanian rule. He thinks it is tragic that in the late 1980s, under the tyranny both Stalinist and Chauvinist, tens of thousands of ethnic Hungarians have fled across the border to Hungary.

The playwright is a friend of a friend, formerly a resident of Nagyvárad and now of Budapest, who gave me a name, an address, and a password. I was told to walk around the block at least three times to make sure that I am not followed by the secret police, and once I identify the playwright, I am to ask whether he still has "the ceremonial sword."

I do as told, and the playwright smiles and nods, recognizing me as someone he can trust. He suggests that we sit down in the cellar rather than in the living room because underground he feels safer talking to a stranger, a foreigner. I understand, I say, and he shrugs and laughs at himself, pointing out that his preference for the subterranean is instinctive and primitive—as well as irrepressible.

The cellar is spacious, and even under the dim light of the sixty-watt bulb authorized by the government's austerity program I can see that the soaring Roman arches of the vaulted ceiling are masterfully laid. But the structure looks too new to have been built by the Romans, or by medieval masons who imitated the Romans and whose patrons plotted to reconstruct that empire's order and unity.

The playwright says the house was built by the magistrate in the most famous blood libel case in Hungarian history: in 1882 the Jews of the village of Tiszaeszlár were accused of killing a young Christian woman, allegedly to mix her blood in the unleavened bread of Passover. The charges of ritual murder, which under the magistrate's directions burgeoned into a conspiracy involving fifteen local Jews, were debated throughout Europe, and it seemed likely that the Jews would be convicted.

The name of the magistrate, József Bary, is well known to me. Living some thirty miles from Tiszaeszlár and sniffing the fumes of the anti-Semitism the case sent over the countryside, my great-grandfather Samuel Schwarcz helped raise money for the defense. He got in his fine carriage and visited every well-to-do Jew in Szabolcs County and a few even beyond. Then he and his friends travelled to Budapest and offered an enormous retainer—my family chroniclers speak of the then unbelievably high sum of ten thousand koronas, then the equivalent of ten times as many of today's dollars—to the country's most famous lawyer, the Gentile nobleman Károly Eötvös. Concerned about possible hostile public reaction, Eötvös was at first reluctant to defend the Jews. But he was eventually swayed by the importance of the case, and as he acquainted himself with the facts, he became convinced that the accused were innocent victims of a blind, murderous fury. He gradually turned into a passionate friend of the Jews.

At the trial, which was covered by newspaper correspondents from a score of countries, the eloquent Eötvös ridiculed the charges and won the case with a flourish. The humiliated magistrate moved to Nagyvárad, to seek his fortune in another county.

The story about my great-grandfather is well received, and my host promptly proposes a toast to the memory of Samuel Schwarcz, a champion of justice. We raise our glasses to drink for justice in the world, for Jew and Gentile, and for Transylvania. The thin cheap wine tastes like the finest champagne.

The highway from Debrecen to Nagyvárad, and from Nagyvárad to the Yugoslav border, is the road once used by the Roman legions, and it passes through the main streets of villages. Their names are familiar to me, though I don't remember which great-uncle married a woman from one village and which cousin bought land in another.

In his last will and testament, dated 1920, my great-uncle Yankev left money to the Jewish communities of fifteen villages in the area: villages where he had studied Torah (which refers both to the five books of Moses and the entirety of traditional lore), met his future wife, or had business dealings. He and his brothers had also donated land and money to turn their ancestral home in the village of Derzs into a fine synagogue. The deed of property transferred in 1906 sternly admonished the local Jewish community that it was duty bound to take good care of the synagogue "forever and ever"; and that if it did not, ownership would revert to the Schwarcz family, "any descendant of which would then be entitled to cancel the gift, and the Derzs Jewish community would be obliged to return it, forfeiting any claim for compensation for its own investments, if any, in the structure."

Who would have questioned then that the synagogues of Szabolcs County would always have Jews to pray in them, and that it was a sound investment to buy lifetime seats by the eastern wall, considered the most prestigious location because it faces Jerusalem, for grandchildren who would be marrying in the 1940s.

There are no more functioning synagogues in Szabolcs County, and no more Jews living in the villages of Hungary and Transylvania, Yugoslavia and Czechoslovakia. Every few years stories circulate about a tractor or a bulldozer or a gardener unearthing a silver menorah or a Torah scroll in a tin box that was buried by some of the six hundred thousand Hungarian Jews killed by the Nazis. There are plenty of hidden Jewish treasures everywhere, people whisper, it will take centuries to uncover the wealth the Jews left behind.

Fortune hunters look for Jewish gold with the same fervor that previous generations dug for the hoard of jewels and precious stones believed to have been buried with Attila, who conquered the land in the fifth century. Scholars believe that his triple coffin—lead, silver, and gold—is underneath the river Tisza somewhere near today's border between Hungary and Yugoslavia. To hide the coffin, the river was first diverted by earthworks built by thousands of foreign slaves and then diverted back, and the slaves were massacred after the completion of their task to guarantee their silence.

Hungarian and Romanian villagers keep items they think might have been owned by a Jew. They will sell a Turkish or Austrian coin as soon as they find it, and they do not usually wait for the right buyer after their plow kicks up pieces of a necklace so old it could have belonged to a Roman patrician. But they hold on to a menorah for years, telling their families that it is wiser to wait for a wealthy Jew who wants it badly, and they will keep as a talisman a scorched fragment of a Hebrew prayer book they picked up, though they say they no longer remember where. But a wealthy Jew is not a frequent visitor in these parts.

Those who interpret dreams in the countryside nowadays say that seeing a Jew in a dream is good luck. It means that the dreamer is on to a fortune, or that his or her hidden talent will soon be uncovered.

I drive a slick red Renault on the same roads where my ancestors once travelled on crude, horse-drawn wagons and elegant carriages. A flock of sheep the color of sand lumbers across the black asphalt, and I stop gladly. I watch them shove and bump one another, even after the shepherd leads them to a new pasture. The car behind me starts honking, and I reluctantly drive on. The pungent odor of the sheep stays with me.

A sign informs me that I have entered Szabolcs County, and soon I park the car next to a century-old walnut tree and get out to admire the sun, which is sinking into a plain as flat as a lake. There is a breeze, and the rustle of the leaves suggests the sound of evening prayers. I sense the presence of my ancestors the way I sense birds hidden in foliage.

Grandparents Róza and Karl Schwarcz in the first years of this century, in front of their house in Gyulaj.

I have been finding myself thinking my ancestors' thoughts and repeating phrases they used. When speaking of them, I add the words, "of blessed memory," after their names. When asked the length of my visit, I answer so, and add, "If God wills it," which is what they would have said.

I pick up a walnut from the ground. Its soft husk is half green, full of live tissue, and half black and dead, and I hear myself muttering the opening words of the Kaddish, the Hebrew prayer for the dead that does not once mention dying or death or the dead, but which helps the soul free itself from the body and rise to a higher sphere. In the Kaddish we "glorify, sanctify, bless, praise, exalt, extol, honor, adore, and laud God's name." The prayer is a wreath of synonyms of praise for the Lord, the God of Our Fathers, and keeps us alive and gives us peace. Suddenly it becomes clear to me that our prayer for the dead is our pledge of allegiance to life.

For the first time in my life I visit Derzs, a small village of less than a thousand souls, and its slightly larger neighbor Gyulaj, which my widowed grandmother Róza and her seven

21

children left tearfully in 1927, after their estate there went bankrupt.

Derzs is where my ancestors settled at least four, and possibly several more centuries ago. They might have lived there when Hungary was still ruled by the House of Árpád, whose kings descended from the legendary tribal chieftain who led his people out of the steppes on the banks of the Volga river and whose horsemen completed in the year 896 their conquest of the land that later became known as the Kingdom of Hungary. Then, as now, Derzs was at the end of a road, a cul-de-sac village. Even today it is half a day's bus ride from the nearest big town, Nyiregyháza.

While other Jews chose to live at busy crossroads to be in a better position to trade and to travel, and to move quickly when threatened by invading armies, murderous mobs, or plain bad times, my ancestors looked for a quiet haven where they could raise wheat and cattle and fruit, and later, sheep and potatoes. Theirs was a hideaway on a land so flat that the ruts left behind by wagon wheels are the lowest points into which rainwater drains.

My ancestors planted trees to anchor the faithless yellow sand that runs off with the wind that blows most of the time. From the early nineteenth century on, they relied on black locust trees. Some of the tallest trees in Derzs today were planted by them, while others sprouted from scattered seeds of the first plantings.

The sunlight filtered by the foliage and refracted by the sand offers a shifting mix of gold and green. The gold has the tint of late-afternoon sunshine that aficionados call old gold to distinguish it from the brassy nouveau riche glitter of newly minted gold. The green is the rampant elemental color of the rainforest, promising growth and vegetation everlasting.

The gold tames and refines the green, and the green shows the gold to its best advantage. Together, the two colors stand for civilization, as it is defined in the poet's meshing of nature and artifice.

The landscape captures me instantly. I was not told how lovely and harmonious it is, and no story about my ancestors' ambition to create a rich dark soil prepared me for the sensation of scooping up a fistful and inhaling its fecundity.

The villagers and I find ourselves speaking the same language of land and time. One man who engages me in conversation is delighted to find out whose grandson I am. He points out perfect squares of plots surrounded by locust trees two to three stories high. He explains that the land once belonged to my grandfather, then the most prominent landowner in the village, who "thus defined what was his."

Now in his seventies, the farmer can identify every piece of real estate that my family owned or leased in the county. I tell him that he is too young to have been an eyewitness. He says that what he knows he heard from his father who worked for my grandfather and used to haul manure every winter, year after year, with two men on the wagon shoveling the stuff to cover the ground which was later plowed. "Your grandfather knew how to improve the land," the villager says, "and he knew how to deal with people. He knew how to bring everything together. He was much liked here, and his name is remembered."

I ask him how and why my family lost its lands. "Your uncles Shumi and Mishi weren't good businessmen," he says, dismissing them as "just like other scions of the landed gentry: light-headed." He also finds fault with advice given by their cousins, whom he knows by name. He has some sharp words for the family lawyer as "the man who took advantage of your problems." But above and beyond every human factor, he blames "the war"—and he means the First World War— when "the world got smashed into pieces, and there was nothing anybody could do to stop that."

The farmer is a hardheaded realist and a Calvinist, which is the minority religion in the village. The majority are Greek Catholics, and their priest, in his fifties and in Derzs only for the past five years, reads Hungarian novels and poetry, and he struggles with books in German, French, and English. He refuses to have anything to do with Russian, even though his forebears and those of his parishioners were Slavs who migrated from the steppes east of the Carpathian mountain range more than a thousand years ago and who followed Byzantine Christianity when the invading Hungarian tribes were still pagans whose shamans sacrificed white horses. The son of a priest and born in a village some ten miles away, he is an amateur historian and archeologist, as well as a dreamer—a species for which Szabolcs County is well known. Dreamers can be as unpredictable as the local birds who fill the air with loud, cheerful twitter one year and keep unaccountably quiet the next.

The priest talks about the forty years of communism as "a tragic era during which an entire generation dropped out of not just religion, but the possibility of a life lived by an ethical code." He tells me he has a plan to bring his flock back to religion, but a few minutes later he sees no hope because the world is breaking up into pieces faster than it can be repaired. Then he tells me that he teaches the history of my family as "an exemplar of loyalty to a faith and a place."

The priest takes me to his church to show me what he calls "our little miracle, which like all miracles is unique and can't be replicated": In shoring up a sinking nave that threatened to bring down the building, workmen dug deep and discovered hitherto unsuspected twelfth century foundations of beaten earth and walls made of laths encased in adobe. Scholars who came from Budapest to study the site now suggest that the structures were damaged by Genghis Khan's hordes in 1241, and that in the centuries that followed, the church went through Romanesque, Gothic, and Baroque phases of rebuilding. Each phase now uncovered offers some feature of beauty—an arched window, or a niche for a patron of the church—which the priest says he had hoped for and even dreamed about but could not prove until the excavation.

I share the priest's enthusiasm for tracing the genesis of his church two, perhaps three centuries deeper into time. He tells me about his argument with his parishioners, who want to see the church covered again with smooth plaster and glossy new paint, and who are firmly against exposing any of the crumbling, medieval brick structures. I agree with him wholeheartedly, and he asks for my permission to cite my opinion to his parishioners. I can't believe my word can carry any weight; he strongly disagrees.

He points proudly to the stone planter on his verandah where he displays some ten skulls, presumed victims of the Mongolian invasion, which he dug up from underneath the sacristy floor installed in the church's Gothic phase. The vivid red blossoms of his geraniums brush against the bleached skulls. Above them is the dense green tangle of a grape arbor, and I say something about how this image affirms life. But I also appreciate his rejoinder, a world-weary quote from the Bible, spoken in the original Hebrew, about the display proving that all is vanity.

He teaches the Hebrew alphabet to his parish children and shows me the primers he is using, which were printed for

Jewish children in the 1930s. He acknowledges that his project is unrealistic—of what possible use can Hebrew be to Greek Catholic villagers? But he interrupts himself in mid-thought: "Must we always be so practical, so down to the mud and dust of the earth? Man must rise above and soar. . . . But Hebrew is tough." He sighs. "Oh God, our shared God, yours and mine, tell us why is the holy language so very, very tough?"

His eyes fill with tears when he mentions my uncle Shumi, who died a year ago and who had sent him the primers. He cannot forgive himself for missing Shumi's funeral, he says, but the bishop summoned him on some silly business he now knows he should have ignored. . . . Shumi, he sighs, that dear man of the dear nineteenth century, used to visit with him and exchange letters with the children, and it is thanks to him that the children, who are almost adults now, are interested not only in the Schwarcz family but in the history of the village.

It is a sunny, languid, timeless village afternoon. The steady drone of honeybees from the priest's kitchen garden is in harmony with the clatter of hammers, trowels, and spades from the church reconstruction. When the workers stop for a snack, one of them crosses the street to offer to share with us their bread, bacon, and onions—all from his home, he assures us, not from any store.

The hours fly as the priest and I talk in the parsonage. Built some two hundred years ago, it is a spacious, pleasant, whitewashed house with nine-foot ceilings. The floor of unvarnished pine planks is worn down and the knots bulge like an old peasant's knuckles. Books, photographs, documents, and files are everywhere, in stacks on the floor and on chairs and in cupboards; letters are spiked on nails in the walls.

The priest and I talk about everything under the sun, as if we knew each other all our lives, and I make a donation for the church, just as my grandfather did before me. My forebears visited the parsonage countless times, just as the priest's predecessors visited my ancestral home, which my grandfather and his brothers rebuilt and turned into a synagogue in 1906. In 1945, two or three young village Jews who survived the Nazis returned home, dismantled the tin roof, dug up the Torah scroll their families had hidden, and sold whatever they could remove and sell quickly, and used the money to make their way to Palestine. The building, made of adobe and plaster, soon collapsed and was later rebuilt with bricks to serve as a kindergarten.

As we stand in front of the parsonage, saying an extended good-bye, villagers come by, and the priest introduces me. Once they hear my first name and whose grandson I am, they promptly call me Károly *bácsi*, the equivalent of Uncle Charles. Even those much older than I address me that way, rather than by my family name preceded by Mister, the appellation villagers normally use for a stranger and for a townsman. They know without asking that I am named after my grandfather. They all know of him, and the connection they make and the honor they extend to me are immediate and unmistakable. In Derzs, where my grandfather was born, and in Gyulaj where he set up his own estate, I am not just his descendant, but his heir and proxy.

I recall what the Talmud says about time: that in the Torah—and by implication, in all matters truly important—there is no "before" and there is no "after," that the trials and triumphs of Abraham, Isaac, and Jacob were recorded not only before they were born but before Creation, and that every Jewish soul who has ever lived or will live was present

in the wilderness of Sinai when Moses accepted the Torah
on their behalf. Such notions would have been manna for
Henry David Thoreau, who, living in wooded hills, thought
of time as a stream to go a-fishing in. But what I see all
around for miles and miles is sand—homogeneous, partic-
ulate, fathoms deep. It dents under the weight of each foot-
step. Its layers are endlessly shuffled by the wind, and each
grain of sand is a fraction of time as measured by an hourglass.
As I think of the skulls and the geraniums sharing space in
the priest's grape arbor, it seems to me that what is illusory
is history, and that it is for the census-taker's convenience
that we limit ourselves to one lifetime, from birth to death.
I hum to myself: linear time is reason's sweet dream.

The fields beckon. Spread out in what is called "the boundary," they are beyond the houses which cling to the two streets
of the village. The road between the village and the fields
suggests a stroll, and each bend offers an invitation to the
next. My feet feel weightless. I look for a sliver of reedy
marsh, known in Szabolcs County as *vadviz*, which translates
as "wildwater." It is a twilight zone between land and water,
and its contours shift from day to day. For a long time I wait
for a shadow to fall suddenly across the water, as still as a
tombstone, even though there is no one and nothing above
to cast it. According to local tradition, that is how the presence of a spirit can be ascertained in broad daylight. The
wind blows from the northeast, from the unseen mountains,
and the cattails that sprouted from seeds which had found
their way to the *vadviz*—not marked on any map—quiver,
bend, and arch, their leaves fluttering like cavalry battle
flags from another century. But I see no shadow that is un-
accounted for.

I am hoping to catch a glimpse of an ancestor of mine on

28

a deserted dirt road, as he sits on the edge by a drainage ditch, stretching his legs in the moist moonlight while he waits for a wayfarer who would wish him good evening, take him for a man still alive, and accept his invitation to halt and to listen to a story. That is what ghosts do, locals believe, and they fear the morose, silent spirit who crouches with knees drawn close to the chin, and the angry one who rattles a rusty chain while walking about, in search of revenge for having been cheated out of a plot of land or abandoned by a husband. But there are also gentle ghosts eager for a visit with the living. One may be troubled by some unfinished business—something of value he buried which he wants to point out to the proper person to dig up—while another is determined to remind the living of a story he treasures but which no one alive remembers anymore.

A ghost should not be interrupted, but he may be asked three questions before he begins to tell his story, which he completes by the time the first cock crows. He then vanishes in the dawn's mist, which is the color of apricots, shuttling back to his grave, passing through hedgerows of elderberry and the ground of the cemetery as if they too were made of mist.

How I wish I had met one of my ancestors and had a chance to ask my questions: when did we get to this part of the earth, what kept us here, and why are we still so attached to it?

The mists I saw swaddled the land, swirled toward the treetops, and then slipped beyond the horizon. But they appeared to be empty, hiding no one I could see.

Local lore also suspects that ghosts lurk in the adobe walls of the taverns where they once stopped off to sip plum brandy from squat, thick-bottomed shot glasses. It is said that some of them can't stay away from the Gypsy tunes they loved and that others eavesdrop to keep up with village gossip. There is no formula for coaxing them out of the walls, which can be more than a foot thick, but at least one necromancer, who is also Szabolcs County's greatest writer, Gyula Krudy, suggested at the beginning of this century that a descendant engaged in a project to the liking of his forebears and pleading for their help might get the ghost of one of them to step out of the wall and sit and talk. Should that ever happen to me, I don't think we would waste our time discussing the present century, with its fallen kings and corrupt bolsheviks, its devastation in the wake of the swastika and the current chaos as the red star finally fades. We would talk instead about what matters: the Torah of tending fruit trees and vineyards and wheat fields, and the art of keeping our children faithful to the covenant of forefather Abraham.

I keep eyeing the walls, whitewashed with quicklime and uneven like sand scoured by the winds. My ancestors, however, have visited me only in my dreams. They were kind and reassuring, and although their measured demeanor seemed to bear all sorts of secrets, they told me no story and answered no question.

I walk the dirt road where relatives and villagers took turns in carrying my grandfather's coffin on a raw, blustery day in March 1920. I pass by the canal, straight as a ruler and paid for by my great-grandfather Samuel, which still drains swamps and protects against flooding. I admire the corn growing all around, smaller than in the United States but just as ornamental with its upright stalk and arching blades. No human is in evidence, and the silence is total, sundered from time to time by the piercing cry of a bird hidden in the fields.

The road is not only the shortest distance between my

grandfather's house and the family cemetery—which is what the Jewish law prescribes for a funeral procession—it is also part of a network of dirt roads that crisscross the country, but which appear on no map. Sometimes a dirt road runs parallel to a paved road, sometimes perpendicular to it, and sometimes there is no visible connection. Faced by churches, taverns, and fine brick homes, the paved roads are the ancient main routes used by armies on the march and government officials collecting taxes. The dirt roads, now flanked by collapsing adobe huts and shacks housing old wine-presses, have served villagers who work in the fields, fugitives seeking a way to safety, as well as defeated armies and secret lovers.

The only Jews still in Derzs are those buried in our family cemetery, which is surrounded by locust trees and wedged in by cornfields. The graves are in precise rows. The headstones erected in the past one hundred years are made of marble and are upright, their Hebrew lettering clear even though the rains have washed out the gold paint. Headstones from the eighteenth century, made of grainy, coarse limestone quarried from nearby, lean to one side or another and crumble at the edges. Still earlier headstones have sunk into the soft sand long ago, and their presence is suggested by a dip in the flat surface. The oldest of them, next to the road, must be several feet in the earth.

A villager in his thirties walks over to find out who the visiting stranger is and what his purpose may be. He introduces himself as the next–door neighbor to the cemetery. As we shake hands, he looks into my eyes, examines my face, then he asks me, and his words float in the air like rose petals: "Aren't you one of our Jews?"

With a lump in my throat, I can only nod and keep nodding.

"Welcome home," he says.

2.

The Man Who Saw an Angel

*How fortunate are the righteous, for they can pass on
their merits to their children.*
A JEWISH SAYING, PARAPHRASING THE TALMUD

In the year 1744, a child was born to an aging couple in
the tiny village of Derzs, in the northeastern pocket of
Hungary's Great Plain. To the north and the east were
the pine-covered Carpathian mountains, and beyond them
Poland and Russia. Derzs was at the end of a road, staggered
with potholes the size of a bucket, that led to the flat, treeless,
arid semi-desert called *puszta* in Hungarian and ended up at
the gate of the rich trading town of Debrecen, where Jews
were allowed to stay during the day but were required to leave
by nightfall.

The child, a boy, was named Baruch, the first word in
countless Hebrew blessings, meaning "blessed." It was his
parents' way of saying how they felt about the arrival of a
child after many years of marriage and after they had given
up all hope of having a child.

Baruch's father earned a modest living leasing a plot of
land from a proud nobleman—a descendant of one of the
seven tribal chieftains who in 896 conquered the land that
later became known as Hungary—who never condescended
to speak to him. The father sold the wheat and the cattle that

Hungarian peasants drink it up in a village inn in the eighteenth century, as shown in a contemporary engraving.

he and his occasional hired hands raised, and he did some trading, mostly with other Jews in nearby villages.

Baruch grew up a wiry, restless, brooding youth. As a small child, he often talked to the Christian villagers, who thought him friendly and smart but a bit odd. At five he told his father he wanted to speak to God. "What would you say?" the surprised parent asked. Baruch promptly replied: "I would ask God, where are you and how did you get there?"

Once, when he was ten, Baruch engaged in conversation the Calvinist preacher of the village. "Is God Jewish?" Baruch asked, and the preacher said God was the God of all peoples and could not be partial to any. It was a polite and friendly answer from a thoughtful man, given after some pondering, but it did not entirely satisfy Baruch. He put the same question to the Jew who was considered the most learned in the village. "Of course God is Jewish," came the confident answer, and for the time being it settled the issue.

Baruch was not yet twenty when he took his father's wagon to neighboring villages and later to the two towns of Szabolcs County, Kálló and Nyiregyháza, where he sold sacks of wheat and an occasional calf, bought salt, pots and pans, bolts of cloth, and nails and paint. But what mattered to him most was a chance to catch a glimpse of the world beyond his village, where nothing ever seemed to happen and where he felt caged. In his midtwenties, he began to go on longer trips. He travelled east, over the narrow, twisting, rock-strewn roads of the Transylvanian mountains, and he visited villages few outsiders ever saw. He wandered through the Great Plain, the country's heartland, which was dusty, hot, and bustling during the summer months, muddy, cold, and morose in the fall and spring, and asleep under a vast goosedown cover of snow in the winter.

Dutifully, but without fervor, Baruch chanted his prayers when he was alone and with other Jews in synagogues. He also peeked into churches and was baffled by their carved and painted images. He carried a hefty stick to defend himself against dogs. "Why do you sic your dogs on me?" he asked the peasants, who either said nothing or cursed him. "Why do we Jews suffer so much?" he asked Jews. "Is there any hope for an improvement in our life before the coming of the Messiah?" Speaking with Christians, he tried to find out the real reasons Jews were hated and persecuted.

The idea of converting to Christianity occurred to him, but he rejected it as cowardly, unworthy, and unthinkable. Whenever he could, he stayed with Jews. On the rare occasions when Christian villagers invited him into their houses, he thanked them but said he preferred to sleep in his wagon.

What drove him were questions to which he could not get satisfactory answers: is there another world of the spirit above and beyond the coarse reality of the visible world? And if the soul is immortal, where does it go after the body's death? Why is prayer—the repetition of the same words over and over again, day after day—so important? Why is the Kaddish, the prayer for the dead, so critical to the soul of the dead? How does it help? In speaking with friends, his father often referred to him as "my Kaddish," meaning that as a son Baruch would say Kaddish after his father's death.

Is it true, could it be true, that a soul sometimes comes back to rejoin the same family or tribe, and perhaps vaguely remembers the earlier life and even retains some physical characteristics from the previous life? Could it be that Jews repeatedly reincarnating as Jews and sometimes returning to the same family account for the instinctive, reflexive, fabled cohesiveness of the Jewish people and the Jewish family?

Baruch liked to roll off his tongue the Hebrew word for reincarnation, *gilgul*. The word had an elemental power, yet sounded as playful as if a child had made it up. He kept thinking about the fact that the words for wheel and wagon also come from the same root, *gilgul*. Wasn't each reincarnation of the soul a wheeling forward on the same journey?

Feeling the pull of both, Baruch worried that he would never find the right balance between the Jewish tradition in which he was raised and the great world outside that fascinated him. But it wasn't only balance that he feared he lacked. He was always reluctant to make a decision. After he struck a business deal, he felt he should have done better. Nor could he decide what he really cared about. Sometimes he was impressed by the simple wisdom of humble peasants who said that injustice and oppression are the basic facts of life and that the world will never change. On other occasions he admired the self-confident enlightenment of dignified, educated noblemen whose polished phrases predicted reforms and progress—a better world. He both respected and detested the Habsburg Empress's soldiers who watched over the empire's many nationalities, protecting them from one another and at the same time suppressing them all.

His parents were worried. Baruch spent his life speaking to strangers and asking strange questions. He was either off to faraway places or thought about going. He was not married.

"A wandering Aramean was my father," Baruch said in his defense, quoting from the Passover story and referring to the patriarch Abraham. "I am a nomad. I can't see myself settling in one place, chained to one house, tethered to one plot of land. I must move on."

One day, when he was in his early twenties, Baruch crossed

the Danube on a ferry and soon was travelling west through hilly countryside. He had never been that far from home. Accustomed to his county's trees, not much taller than the houses in his village and never too many of them, he was awed by the trees he faced. The size of belltowers, the trees formed an endless and seemingly uninhabited forest.

But he had heard of bandits living in the forest whose friends and accomplices were wild men of the axe who felled trees, split the wood, sold it to townspeople, and were drunk every night. He remembered village storytellers describing mad hermits, foul sorceresses, mischievous elves, and trickster trolls who lived in caves and hollow trees or underneath the roots of ancient stumps. Baruch had not paid much attention to the stories, but it seemed to him now that anything was possible in the dense shade. "We Jews are children of the desert," he thought to himself. "We don't even have names for the creatures that lurk in the woods."

The smooth gray bark of beech trees had a ghostly, whitish sheen and black markings like letters of an unknown script warning of dangers ahead. It was cold and he was shivering. He feared not only bandits and evil spirits, he feared the forest itself.

It was late into the evening when he saw some flickering lights ahead, and soon an inn materialized out of the darkness. He heard angry shouts and the crash of heavy objects, but he entered. He saw four staggering peasants hitting one another with whatever they could get hold of: chairs, wine bottles, wooden tables. They were drunk and reducing the inn to a shambles.

Baruch also noticed a woman weeping softly in a dark corner. "Who are you?" Baruch asked. Her small frame was enveloped in a rough woolen shawl, and she seemed more child than woman.

She did not answer.

Baruch inquired where the inn's owner was.

"My husband, Reb Itzig, is the owner," the woman replied, adding the term of respect "Reb," or Master, to the first name Itzig, which would have been sufficient. "Reb Itzig is in the back room, studying the Talmud."

Though he had never been in a brawl before, Baruch jumped into the fray. He separated and disarmed the peasants, who offered little resistance and lay down on the earthen floor, where they were soon asleep.

He found the owner reading a book. Baruch waited until he saw the man turn the page. He then respectfully inquired if he might have a word with him.

The innkeeper had no objection.

Baruch asked him if he had heard the commotion in the inn and if he had any idea how much damage the peasants had caused.

The innkeeper sighed and said he could not be concerned with such worldly matters.

"But isn't the inn yours?" Baruch asked, puzzled.

"Yes, the inn belongs to me," the man said. "I inherited it from my parents of blessed memory. My wife takes care of the few customers who come by. But I study the Talmud, which is all that interests me. Much to my sorrow, I am all alone, and it has been at least a year since a Jew has been here and studied with me."

Baruch accepted the indirect invitation to study, and Reb Itzig immediately began reading aloud.

For Baruch, the text seemed as dense and overwhelming as the forest surrounding the inn. He asked questions, more

and more questions, and in the answers Reb Itzig offered he
could only find more questions.

But Reb Itzig relished coping with Baruch's questions.
Again and again, he singled out the critical words from the
Hebrew and the Aramaic, and he pointed out the reasons for
the differences between the original text and the interpretative
commentaries by the various rabbis.

Baruch was astounded by the depth of the innkeeper's
learning and his ability to arrive at the essence of a passage
while still taking note of each small detail. Soon Baruch
stopped asking questions. Dutifully, he read the text together
with Reb Itzig and listened to his explanations. They stopped
for prayer when dawn was breaking through a darkness deepened by the towering, straight-trunked beeches. As Reb Itzig's voice soared, Baruch found he could not keep up and
was losing his voice. Reb Itzig suggested they stop and get
some rest.

Baruch was exhausted, but he could not fall asleep in the
inn's tiny guest quarters. The forest and the peasants, Reb
Itzig and the Talmud raced through his mind, and he tried
to deduce their meaning. Finally, he got up, walked out of
his room and into Reb Itzig's, and saw that the innkeeper
was already studying. This time, Baruch did not wait for Reb
Itzig to turn the page.

"I have a suggestion for you, Reb Itzig," he said. "I'll go
to the nearest town, sell your inn, and I'll take you and your
wife with me to my village, which is small and far away but
has some decent, God-fearing Jews. I do not have the authority to invite you on behalf of the community, but there
has been much talk about finding a teacher for the boys, and,
who knows, one day we may be able to afford a rabbi. I know
that you are the right man for my village."

Reb Itzig said he would be happy to go anywhere—anywhere—as long as he could study the Talmud with other Jews. He told Baruch to sell the inn at whatever price.

Baruch harnessed his horse and drove deeper into the forest for several hours before he came upon a small town. It was market day, and the first man he talked to expressed interest in the inn and agreed to buy it at the high price Baruch quoted but had intended only as the asking price. The contract was quickly drawn up, and by evening Baruch brought the buyer over to the inn. Reb Itzig barely glanced at the papers before signing them, and let his wife count the money.

Astonished and exhilarated by the ease and the speed of the day's events, and feeling both tired and triumphant, Baruch that night threw himself into Talmud study. He felt for the first time that he understood the point of what he was reading. He focused on each critical phrase, and he recognized the theme around which the phrases were ordered. He balanced facts and opinions, the text and the commentaries, and found such a balancing act a most comforting posture. Words rolled off his tongue before he thought them through, and his thoughts made sense. Reb Itzig smiled and told Baruch that he seemed to have acquired much wisdom overnight.

As dawn broke the next day, Baruch put Reb Itzig and his wife and their few belongings on his wagon and they began the long journey out of the deep forest, over the hill country, across the Danube and then through the dusty roads of the Great Plain.

Reb Itzig and Baruch talked.

With patience and precision, Reb Itzig answered Baruch's questions one by one. Listening to the learned man, Baruch had the same feeling of fulfillment he had while harvesting apples and pears from the trees around his parents' house. He was happy to discover that Reb Itzig was sympathetic to his ideas about Jews reincarnating as Jews, although Reb Itzig thought that finding one's role and place in one's current life is more important than trying to identify previous incarnations. In fact, God is most merciful and compassionate, Reb Itzig argued, in blotting out one's memories of former lives so that a person wouldn't be forever moping about a better life in the past or, prompted by a sudden elevation in status, become overconfident. But what really matters is to remember one's ancestors, Reb Itzig said. A son must say Kaddish for a father so the father's soul may soar and reach the Almighty. The Kaddish is a link in a chain that goes back to Jacob, Isaac, and Abraham, and the chain must not be broken. Having a Jewish soul means nourishing that continuity and being nourished by it.

Reb Itzig and Baruch chanted the prayers together, and Baruch was astonished at how soon they reached the rippling sand dunes of Szabolcs County. As soon as they arrived in Derzs, Baruch called all the adult male Jews together—who numbered at most ten, the quorum for prayer and community required by Jewish law—and introduced Reb Itzig. It did not take long for the Jews to discover that the newcomer was exceedingly wise in the ways of the Talmud. They hired him as the teacher for their children and they could hardly wait to tell their friends in neighboring villages what a treasure they had acquired.

Weeks, months, years went by, and Baruch did not leave the village even once. His restlessness had vanished. Every evening he studied Talmud with Reb Itzig, and during the day he took care of his business and became moderately prosperous.

41

His parents were delighted that his strange journeys were over and that the questions which had troubled him were now answered. He married and within a year became the father of a son, whom he named Itzig after his teacher and friend.

The community grew, and it asked Reb Itzig to serve as its first rabbi. He accepted. Jews from surrounding villages came to hear him talk.

One unusually warm early spring morning, Baruch could not keep his mind on his work. The earth just thawed had a strange smell he had never smelled before, and he was over-come by a fear that he was doing something wrong, or that perhaps something terrible was happening in the village.

Out in the fields, with his hired men working alongside him, he could not get his mind off a passage in Genesis: was the land cursed after the Fall of Man? If work on the land is cursed, how can the land and its fruit be blessed? Unable to come up with an answer and shivering despite the warm weather, he went to see Reb Itzig. It was not an hour for visits, but Baruch was such a good friend of the rabbi that he didn't think twice about it.

He knocked on Reb Itzig's door. Hearing no answer, he entered the house.

He could hardly believe what he saw. As usual, Reb Itzig was hunched over a book. But this time he had no clothes on.

Such nakedness was more than inappropriate: it was a scandalous violation of the Jewish law of modesty. Except for immersion in the ritual bath, it is a sin for a pious Jew to be uncovered during the day. At the very least, he must wear a ritual undergarment.

Yet the saintly, learned rabbi in front of him was as naked as an animal. Was he mocking the holiness of the book he was reading by having no clothes on? Might he be practicing

some sort of black magic? Was he a secret heretic, abusing
and subverting the hidden powers of the holy book for some
nefarious purpose of his own as some Jews, denounced and
disowned by the rabbis, were said to be doing across the
mountains in Poland?

In a moment, Baruch weighed his dark suspicions and
dismissed them all. He knew—he knew for certain—that Reb
Itzig was a pure soul.

Baruch covered his eyes with his hands and exclaimed: "I
saw an angel! I saw an angel, and I thank the Almighty for
letting me see an angel!"

Then he turned around, left the room, carefully closed the
door behind him, and sat down on the bench in front of the
house.

It occurred to Baruch that he might have been dreaming
while awake. Could it be that the vision of the naked rabbi
reading a holy book was just a hallucination on a strange day
of unseasonal heat—a nightmare? Or, God forbid, did Reb
Itzig die suddenly, and did Baruch see the ghost of a man
who still had to finish studying a page of Talmud?

Time passed—perhaps hours, perhaps only minutes.

At last, Reb Itzig came out of the house. He was dressed
in his usual black coat and trousers, and white shirt. He sat
next to Baruch.

"I was born a child of aged parents," Reb Itzig began his
explanation, "and my skin has always been extremely sensitive. It sometimes gets to be so uncomfortable that I cannot
bear the touch of any clothing—be it cotton, wool, or linen.
The itching is the worst when it starts getting warm. I feel I
must shed all my clothing, or else I go crazy.

"This sickness is my dark, dark secret. Because you did
not think ill of me when you had every reason to do so, and

43

because you did not humiliate me in my shame and in my misfortune, I will pray to the Almighty, the God of Our Fathers, that you live in peace and in good health until the fullness of human days, one hundred and twenty years."

Baruch accepted Reb Itzig's explanation and kept his secret. They continued to study together, and Baruch gained in wisdom. He became known as Reb Itzig's disciple, and after Reb Itzig reached a ripe old age and died, people went to Baruch for advice.

Baruch grew older and older, and people began to wonder if the Angel of Death might have forgotten him.

The Empress Maria Theresa, under whose reign Baruch was born, died in Vienna in 1780, when he was thirty-six. She said that Jews were "worse than the plague" and she issued edicts expelling them from Prague and Vienna, and it took enormous bribes to talk her out of similar expulsions elsewhere. The only way she would grant an audience to Jews was from behind a partition.

But her son, Josef II, was a man of the Enlightenment and a suspected freemason who raised the judicial status of Jews to a "tolerated minority" in order to "render them more useful to the state." An enthusiastic administrator, he decreed in 1781 that henceforth all Jews in his empire must take up proper family names, and he set up offices where all citizens, including Jews, had to be registered, and their births and deaths promptly and precisely accounted for. Because he declared German to be the language of civilization, while banning Hebrew and Yiddish as the languages of communal records, he expected Jews to adopt German names. Thus Baruch became Baruch Fisch.

On his deathbed in 1790, Josef II stunned his subjects by revoking his reforms—except for the Jewish laws.

The old order was changing, the world was turning upside down. In faraway Paris, people had stormed the palaces of the rich and killed their king and queen. Then the heir of that revolution, Napoleon Bonaparte, defeated the Habsburg Emperor Franz and married his daughter. The Jews of Europe and the Middle East were both pleased and puzzled when the Corsican upstart who crowned himself emperor emancipated all the Jews living in the lands he conquered and called together a Sanhedrin of wise men to make new laws for Jews. In every corner of the Jewish world, rabbis debated whether he was a precursor to the Messiah or a cunning enemy scheming to lure Jews out of the synagogue and into secular society. Some of the most respected rabbis of Eastern Europe prayed for his success. It was said that in his dreams Napoleon kept seeing a red-bearded Jew who pointed in the direction his armies should march through Poland and Russia. But other rabbis, equally respected, prayed for his defeat, and in the end he was undone by an alliance of forces fearful of change. Or, as Victor Hugo put it, "God got bored with him."

With Napoleon in exile, the Holy Alliance of Habsburgs and Romanoffs, Hohenzollerns and Bourbons restored the old feudal order. But in Hungary, there was more and more talk of freeing the serfs, and the noblest of the nobility saw the need to grant judicial equality for all classes of people, including Jews. The monarchs resisted, and the result was a wildfire of revolutions in 1848 in Vienna and Pest, in Paris and Berlin, in Prague and Milan. The House of Habsburg shook in its foundations. And had it not been for the armies of Czar Nicholas I, the Habsburgs would have lost their Hungarian possessions.

Thousands of Hungarian Jews, including members of Baruch Fisch's family, joined the rebels, and in the repression that followed, the Jewish community had to pay a large fine for defying the emperor.

Baruch Fisch lived through it all, ensconced in his native village, far from the towns where great men debated the great reforms and far from the highways where the armies marched to crush or shield the *ancien régime*.

Baruch Fisch welcomed the reforms of Josef II, but he didn't like the imperial nationalism the monarch espoused. He paid little attention to Napoleon and even less to Napoleon's enemies. "This too shall pass," he said, citing a talmudic sage. "Only the Torah is eternal."

He read his holy books and led his congregation in prayer. His parents had died before the end of the eighteenth century. His wife passed away in the first decade of the nineteenth century. Their only son, Itzig, was the grandfather of grown men and women.

One summer morning word came to Baruch Fisch that his son had fallen ill. He went to see him, and when he entered the house, he heard a flapping of wings. He knew it was the Angel of Death, come to take away his son's soul.

Baruch Fisch whispered: "Long, long ago, a learned man of blessed memory, Reb Itzig, promised to pray that I live to the fullness of human days, one hundred and twenty years. It seems to me that Reb Itzig's prayer was heard, because I am now one hundred and nineteen years old. May I ask that the remaining one year of my life be given to my son, so that I will not have to do something as sad and as unnatural as saying Kaddish at the funeral of my only son?"

The Angel of Death did not reply.

Baruch Fisch held Itzig's hand, which felt as cold as ice, and he prayed for his son, whose beard was as white and as long as his own.

Then Baruch Fisch got on his wagon and drove around the fields where he had worked all his life, and he inspected the crops. He prayed at his parents' graves, and he said good night to all the adults and children who called him grandfather. He visited with his friends. It was close to midnight when he got home and went to bed.

Next morning, his son Itzig woke up, healthy and restored. But Baruch Fisch was dead.

Itzig Fisch, himself close to a hundred, lived one more year, and when he was buried, next to his father, his grandchildren were accompanied by their grandchildren—and the youngest of them, four years old, was my grandfather.

Isaac Taub, the Rabbi of Kálló,
in an early nineteenth-century painting.

3.

A Dark Night, a Dream, and a Blessing

Nothing is miraculous about a miracle except that it comes when it does. The east wind has probably swept bare the ford in the Red Sea hundreds of times, and will do so again hundreds of times. But that it did this at a moment when the people in their distress set foot in the sea—that is the miracle.
FRANZ ROSENZWEIG, "Judah Ha-Levi"

There was a time not long ago in the Old World when a Jew cultivating his own land was as rare as a black swan. Wanderers from country to country, Jews were expelled by a king's decree or by a mob's fury, or, fearful of both, they were on the lookout for a safer, less troubled place to live. As recently as a hundred years ago, they were forbidden to own land in some countries, and where they were not, they were afraid to buy land because they could not strap it on their backs if they had to leave.

To explain how my ancestors began an enduring love affair with the land and why little by little they bought more and more of it, and cherished it in ways far beyond the way one usually values the source of one's livelihood, my family chroniclers point to a certain young man, six generations removed from mine, who was born toward the middle of the eighteenth century. At that time, Jews in the Hungarian part of the Habsburg empire, numbering some twenty thousand souls and often as transient as flocks of birds, were considered so insignificant that the law did not require them to have last names. When paying taxes, lending money to a feudal lord, or signing a contract to lease a tavern, a Jew was known by his first name, followed by his father's. But since that was the custom in the world of the Bible as well, he didn't think of it as an indignity.

The young man's first name was Daniel, but his father's name has disappeared in the mists of time. Daniel had a lighthearted, cheerful disposition and a friendly, open nature. In his village of Derzs, where everyone followed in his father's or mother's footsteps and the smallest detour was suspect, he was for trying out new ideas. "It will work if we give it a try," was his favorite sentence. According to our family tradition, he was the first entrepreneur in Szabolcs County, if not in the entire eastern part of the country, to raise a flock of sheep for wool rather than meat, starting in the 1770s.

For months before taking his father's wagon to sell the fleece of the first season at the great market of the capital city of Buda—which was not as yet united with Pest, across the Danube river—Daniel was talking about the joy of spending the nights on the road stretched out on top of his sacks of wool. It was going to be a great adventure, he told family and friends, he would look around and listen, and bring home new ideas. His parents were worried because travelling to Buda took more than a week, passing through the Great Plain was dangerous, and their son had never been so far away. But they thought it was no use trying to stop him.

On the first night, which was moonless and cloudy, as well as darker than he remembered any other night, Daniel stopped by a spacious, barnlike structure covered with a sturdy reed roof and open on the sides. It was an institution left behind by the Turks, who called it a caravanserai, where for a small amount of money, a man and his horse and wagon could find safety from bandits and shelter from rain and snow. Nevertheless, Daniel dreamt of thieves and highwaymen, ice storms and hot winds. It was something of a relief when he woke in the middle of the night to the sound of muffled cries.

He got up, and in the nearly empty caravanserai he found a young man moaning and groaning, as if in pain, twisting and turning on the thick layer of straw that covered the earthen floor. The young man wore the then-customary garb of Jews: trousers gathered into white stockings under the knee, a knee-length jacket made of black gabardine, black shoes with buckles, and a wide-rimmed black hat trimmed with dark beaver fur. He seemed to be tormented by a nightmare.

Daniel, who had been taught that one should wake a person who is troubled by a nightmare, woke the young man. He offered a drink of water from his canteen and asked if there was anything wrong.

The man said he was feeling ill and miserable, but that his condition was no worse than usual. "At night I have seizures and visions," he said, his voice heavy with sadness and suffering. "But since that is the will of the Almighty, I must not complain."

Daniel suggested that the man, who seemed to be about his age, come to his wagon and enjoy the comfort of his sacks of wool, which were soft as a mattress and warm as a blanket. He was glad to have a chance to explain that the wool came from the flock of sheep he had raised himself, and that they were all healthy, wonderful animals with fine fleece.

The man accepted the invitation. He found the wool indeed soft and warm, and there was plenty of room for both of them on the wagon. Still, he turned and turned but could not fall asleep. Daniel asked if there was anything he could do to help.

The man said he had walked all day, starting at dawn, and that he should be too tired for anything but the deep sleep

51

of exhaustion, yet his worries were so numerous and so powerful and insistent that they either kept him awake or gave him bad dreams as soon as he fell asleep.

"What are your worries?" Daniel asked.

The moon slipped out from behind the clouds and Daniel suggested they go for a walk around the caravanserai. In his family, he said, talking while taking a stroll was considered the best way to think.

The man agreed. He explained that he had just completed his studies as a rabbi in one of the small villages in Poland, north of Hungary. He was on his way to the town of Kálló, still many miles away, to apply for his first job.

Daniel thought it was wonderful to be a rabbi and that Kálló, then the capital of Szabolcs County, was a fine town. It was some fifteen miles from his village, and he had once visited it with his father. The Jewish community there was large and strong, with close to a hundred souls, and a rabbi there would have a good life.

"But I am much too young to get the position of rabbi," came the reply. "I am barely over twenty years old. Kálló is a rich community, and it can easily afford an older, experienced rabbi, even a famous one. I don't know a single soul in Kálló, and I don't even have an introduction to someone in the congregation. If I were a sober, rational person, I would not be applying for the job."

Daniel said that some of Kálló's Jews were indeed relatively well off, but that often each person of means had his own choice for a rabbi. It could be that different factions wanted different rabbis, and a young rabbi whom none of them knew could be just the right compromise whom everybody could agree on without hurting the feelings of someone important in the congregation. But even if for some reason he did not get the job, he could still be a teacher of the children, and that was a good way to earn prestige and influence and become the rabbi one day.

The rabbi said he appreciated Daniel's optimism, and it was quite likely that Daniel was right in his line of reasoning, but he had doubts of a deeper nature as well. "Should I really be a rabbi?" he asked. "Am I really meant to be a rabbi?" A lifetime of study did not appeal to him, he said. He liked a more active life than reading the Talmud all day, however praiseworthy that was, or presiding over weddings and funerals, regardless of the importance of the synagogue or the devotion of the congregation.

Moreover, he said, the idea of being shackled to one synagogue made him apprehensive. When he studied in Poland, and in Moravia before that, he went from one rabbinical school to another, always attracted by the promise of another teacher and interested in mixing with another group of students. But he was also lured by the endless ribbon of the road. He had once had a dream that somewhere off the main highway there was a winding, narrow road that led to a small, quiet village no outsider knew, and that village, with an abundance of beautiful trees and birds, held the key to the secret of happiness.

"I live in a tiny village off the main road that no one ever notices," said Daniel. "The few outsiders who visit are those who have already been there."

"You are fortunate to be living in such a village," said the rabbi. "Don't leave it."

Daniel pondered over the advice. Then he asked: "What is it that made you want to become a rabbi?"

"Just about the only thing that commends me for the rabbinate is a good singing voice," the rabbi replied, but his voice sounded tired and thin. "The test in Kálló should determine not just whether I would be the rabbi of that particular community, but whether I should be a rabbi at all."

Daniel said he too was at a crossroads. He too had just passed the age of twenty, and it was only the previous year that he persuaded his father, who rented land from a nobleman, to buy three dozen sheep and to raise them for wool. He was on his first trip to sell the fleece and he had taken his father's wagon and best horse. "Would it pay to raise sheep for wool?" Daniel asked. "I think so, and that's what I tell my father, but sometimes I doubt it. The fact is nobody can be sure. And who can tell besides the Almighty if I will be good at raising sheep and selling the fleece?"

Like the rabbi, Daniel, too, had some deeper worries. "Tell me, rabbi, whoever has heard of a Jew working on the land?" he asked, and now his voice was plaintive, and heavy with doubt. "Should a Jew ignore our sad experience of expulsions and try to buy land and raise animals on it and cultivate it? Tell me, rabbi, answer my question: should a Jew work on his own land?"

"Yes, a Jew may buy land," the rabbi said, his voice suddenly strong. "Of course, at the moment the law won't permit us. But the law will change." He had heard that Crown Prince Josef was unlike other Habsburgs and most unlike his mother, the Empress Maria Theresa, who had always hated Jews, even more than she hated Protestants. But Josef was a reformer, a free-thinker who favored diversity. "According to the rabbi in Poland I studied under," said the rabbi, "Prince Josef believes that Jews should no longer be restricted to the professions of trade but ought to be given the freedom to choose any enterprise, any business, to help build a more prosperous empire. And why shouldn't a Jew work on the

land? Weren't our ancestors in the Bible shepherds and farmers? Didn't they excel as shepherds and as farmers?"

Daniel said he had never confided to anyone that in early
spring his soul trembled at the beauty of green fields freshly
sprouted and that sometimes he felt like embracing certain
trees as if they were scrolls of the holy Torah. In the synagogue, his heart beat faster every time he heard the Torah
described as "the tree of life." He liked to pick up a handful
of loose dirt just plowed and knead it with his fingertips and
inhale it, as if it were the fragrant spice one sniffed at the
end of Shabbos to remember the specialness and the richness
of the holy day that is set above all others. "I love the soil,"
he said, "and I want to own and take care of my own land."

The rabbi said it was not wrong for a Jew to have such
feelings. On the contrary, Daniel's feelings must be similar
to those of Abraham, Isaac, and Jacob, as well as David and
the prophets. True, they lived in our homeland, in the Land
of Israel, given to us by the Almighty. But, the rabbi continued, and he himself was surprised by what he said, the
land is portable. Just as the synagogue, which may be built
anywhere in the world, became a portable Temple after the
Romans destroyed the Holy Temple in Jerusalem, the land
too has become portable since we lost the Holy Land. Wherever we are, the Almighty expects us to be good stewards of
the land.

The rabbi had great hopes for the nineteenth century, only
a few years away: a new and better world was being born,
and redemption, the time of the Messiah, was fast approach-
ing. The Messiah would not come in the darkest moments of
our history, he argued, for instance, during the Inquisition.
The Messiah will come at the edge of the dawn of an enlight-
ened age which recognizes the equality of all people. The

rabbi's voice was passionate when he declared: "The Messiah must come in our days, in our lifetime."

"You are the first person I know to bring such good tidings," Daniel said. "You have made me feel certain that what I am doing is right and proper, and that I am not straying from our tradition, but going back to it. You are an inspiring man. Indeed, you are a rabbi! You are my rabbi!"

There was a pause after Daniel's outburst. Then the rabbi said, slowly and softly, "I must tell you I am seldom so self-confident. In fact, this is the first time I have been so certain about a question that someone puts to a rabbi. Nor have I had much experience being asked a question the way a rabbi is asked a question. But your courage in testing what is uncertain has made me feel certain."

As they walked back to the wagon, Daniel said he had a request: "You said you have a good singing voice. I don't, much to my sorrow, but I love to listen to someone who has a good voice. Promise me that you will sing a song in the morning."

"I will do so with all my heart," the rabbi said. "Now I wish you a good night. May you dream a good dream." As soon as Daniel said "Thank you," he was asleep, and so was the rabbi.

Daniel had a dream.

He was walking across a broad sunlit meadow covered with thick, tall grass. From it, a sheep emerged and rubbed against him. It had long fleece and its body was unusually long, so long that the sheep wrapped itself in a circle around Daniel's legs. Soon he was surrounded by many more sheep with similar long bodies, and they milled around him in a circle that kept getting larger. He looked up and noticed a house that was very much like his parents' house. As he walked toward it, the house grew a wing on one side and a room was added to the other end. He saw children running out of the house, and then men and women. Many people of all ages came out of the house and walked over to the meadow. They were talking, laughing, singing. Then a shaggy horse with long, long hair appeared, and it snuggled up to him. Suddenly the horse was pulling a wagon, and he jumped on the wagon and rode for a long time on twisting dirt roads with wheatfields on both sides, as far as the eye could see.

Daniel woke up shortly after dawn smiling. "So you had a good dream," said the rabbi, looking at him. Daniel asked how the rabbi had slept, and the rabbi said he felt rested and was eager to get on with his journey.

First, they chanted the morning prayers. The rabbi prayed with great fervor, as if speaking directly to the Almighty. Then he sang a song about David the shepherd king, and the song was so beautiful that Daniel's eyes filled with tears. The rabbi's voice was a robust, resonant bass and he addressed the song to Daniel, who felt that this was a moment he had been waiting for.

Daniel, who was supposed to travel west to Buda, told the rabbi that he would first take the road to the east, to Kálló. The rabbi protested, but Daniel insisted that a rabbi contending for a job must not be tired from walking and should not be seen arriving on foot like a pauper. On the way to Kálló, Daniel told the rabbi his dream.

"Your should remember and treasure your dream last night, my friend Daniel," the rabbi said. "What your dream means is that wealth and honor and happiness will come to you, that you will have many descendants who will have wealth and

57

honor and happiness, and that God will favor you with a long and good life."

When the first houses of Kálló appeared on the horizon, the rabbi asked Daniel to stop the wagon. "May God bless you and all your descendants," he said. "May God help you in your present venture and in all those ventures that will surely follow. For the courage you have displayed in starting your enterprise and for the kindness you showed me, I will pray to the Almighty, the God of Our Fathers, that your seed may be as blessed and as numerous as Abraham's and that you may be as successful in raising animals as Jacob."

The rabbi cited the Prophet Amos: "And I will plant them upon the land and they shall no more be pulled out of the land which I have given them, saith the Lord, thy God." Finally, he said: "May the Lord bless you and favor you and all your descendants who keep the laws of Moses and work on the land."

The two young men said good-bye to each other in front of Kálló's synagogue.

The rest of Daniel's journey was uneventful. After a week, he arrived safely in the market town of Buda. He sold all his wool, and the price they fetched was higher than anybody in his village had considered possible.

In the years that followed, Daniel raised more sheep and sold their fleece at good prices. Like the biblical Jacob, that most crafty and meticulous shepherd, Daniel paid attention to improving the quality of his flock. His sheep were well fed and well cared for, and their fleece was always full and thick.

He also became a landowner. If our family chroniclers are right, he was the first Jew who acquired an estate in the northeastern part of Hungary, if not in the entire country, sometime in the first years of the nineteenth century, long before the reform parliament in 1840 declared it legal for a Jew to own land. How he did that is unclear, but my savviest relatives offer two likely explanations: the remoteness of Daniel's village of Derzs and the popularity he enjoyed.

Many of Daniel's descendants stayed on the land and resisted the temptations of city life and trade and industry, as well as the prestige offered by such professions as medicine and law. They loved the land, and the land returned their love.

The rabbi's blessing worked for more than a hundred and forty years and for some six generations. It did its magic as long as Daniel's descendants working on the land also kept the laws of Moses—the many commandments and rules decreed by the Bible and the Talmud, ranging from the kind of meat that is acceptable for eating to the abstention from all manner of work on the seventh day, Shabbos, from sunset on Friday to sunset on Saturday. One may argue that the blessing is still at work, for many of my relatives who settled in Israel are farmers, and they are successful. They do not, however, observe the laws of Moses.

But what is a blessing? What is its magic?

A blessing comes from the core of the faith, which is the hard conviction that God is just and fair, and rewards those who live according to what tradition calls the Right Way. Usually a blessing is dispensed as an advance payment to a promising youth who is thus encouraged to prove himself or herself. A blessing may come directly from God, as in Abraham's case, and be then handed down as an invaluable, indivisible, and unique gift to one particular favorite son—from Abraham to Isaac, and from Isaac to Jacob. But after Jacob favored Joseph over his brothers, success as well as strife and suffering increased and multiplied. In the end, the dying Jacob blessed all his twelve sons more or less equally,

while reserving a special preference for Joseph and his sons—
and the eldest son, Judah.

In the post-biblical era, the rabbi, serving as the middle-
man between God's grace and a human being's aspirations,
may be moved to ask God to confer a blessing on a person
as a way to repay a kindness or to help out someone who
deserves help, or both. This trade in favors sweetens the
game of blind chance and ruthless competition that so often
seems to make up reality but which in fact is merely the
cynic's world. There is only good fortune, and nothing else,
said the pagan Roman. The pious Jew has always disagreed.
A blessing is a hand on the shoulder or an arm around the
shoulder. It is an assurance that everything will turn out
right—*y'h'yeh tov*, as it is said in the original Hebrew. Don't
worry, I am with you.

How and why my family lost the blessing given in the
1770s is a matter of dispute. Did my uncles and cousins lose
their lands after they stopped observing the many rules of the
Jewish faith, the condition—the *tnai*—of the blessing's promise of prosperity? But that condition was set by the rabbi. In
delivering the blessing, did God accept the rabbi's condition?
What about the despoliation of our lands during and after the
First World War, and the unparalleled devastation by the
Nazis? Didn't they negate, even cancel, such notions as God's
good will, which was the very premise of the blessing?

Perhaps that blessing was tied to a time and a place, valid
only in the ordered world that was shattered by the First
World War. Or it may be that the blessing simply wore out,
as it was eventually meant to.

What became of the rabbi?

Tradition has it that he was first hired as a teacher of

children and then, after a few years, in 1781, elected rabbi of the community of Kálló and chief rabbi of Szabolcs County at the same time.

By the standards of his day, or even of our day, Isaac Taub, known throughout Hungary and in the lands adjacent to it as the Miracle-making Rabbi of Kálló, or, simply, the Rabbi of Kálló, was a most unconventional rabbi. He took long walks in the countryside, sometimes accompanied by another Jew, as custom demanded, but sometimes all by himself, which was considered ill-advised because he might have come upon temptations and dangers he would not have been able to cope with by himself. He sometimes disappeared for days on mysterious errands, riding a wagon and roaming the highways and the back roads. He took naps in the shade of certain trees in the hope that he would dream important dreams: dreams that would point in the direction he or his petitioners should follow, dreams that would open gates hitherto closed, dreams that would explain problems he could not resolve in the light of day.

He visited orchards, particularly when they bloomed; he spoke with those who pruned the trees so he could better understand Jewish tradition, which regards the orchard as a metaphor for Paradise. Unlike other rabbis of his generation who knew Yiddish and Hebrew but only a little, if any, Hungarian, he spoke a folksy, colorful Hungarian. He mixed with Gentiles. He joined shepherds and fishermen at their campfires, and he sat with peasants in taverns. He learned songs from them, and he sang with them just as he sang in the synagogue, with all his heart.

Jewish scholarship lists Rabbi Taub as a disciple of the Baal Shem Tov, the first and perhaps the greatest of the rabbis classified as chassidic, which translates as burning with devotion and drawn to that which is beyond the rational, as opposed to mainstream Judaism which focused on the legalistic and emphasized the rational. After their deaths, the temptation to link the two rabbis was difficult to resist. Isaac Taub was nine when the Baal Shem Tov died in 1760, and some of Rabbi Taub's followers contended that the Baal Shem Tov had once instructed him. Another version of the story claims that shortly before his death, the Baal Shem Tov addressed a letter to a little boy and that, mysteriously, the letter was delivered many years later, after the little boy became the famous Rabbi of Kálló.

The two rabbis lived parallel lives. Both were born poor and were orphaned at an early age. Both worked in menial jobs and then wandered from one rabbinical school to another, seemingly uncertain of their calling and even resisting it, and then wandering from one village to another. Both sought to relieve the misery of Jewish lives, rather than to add more volumes to Jewish learning. Both prayed for the coming of the Messiah with a fervor matched only by the intensity of their appeals to God to help out poor Jews in trouble. Both refrained from writing and discouraged their disciples from recording their words and deeds, and, as a result, we have a wealth of stories about them framed and embroidered by their followers.

For my ancestors, the Baal Shem Tov was the great beacon at the top of the Carpathian mountains which glowed from a great distance, but Rabbi Taub from the nearby town of Kálló was the candle that spread its light in their homes every Friday night.

What kind of a man was the Rabbi of Kálló?

One of his congregants, a pious tailor interviewed by a

writer toward the end of the nineteenth century, described
him as "tall, powerfully built, with a high forehead and with
intelligent eyes that always smiled." He was not a perpetually
angry prophet inveighing against sin and issuing bans, but a
compassionate, trusting friend whose faith was contagious.

He surprised Jewish visitors from other lands who came to
his dinner table Friday night by singing a traditional Hebrew
melody followed by a Hungarian folk song. He praised Josef
II, the Habsburg emperor who accepted Jews as citizens, but
he also publicly criticized Josef's attempt to tighten Vienna's
control over Hungary. After Josef's death in 1790, he made
friends with a nobleman, one of the Hungarian conspirators
who sought independence. Risking an official reprimand if
not imprisonment, the Rabbi of Kálló mourned his friend in
one of his sermons and spoke openly of his sympathy for the
conspirators after they were beheaded in 1795 in the last
medieval ceremony of its kind, on a meadow underneath
Buda's Castle Hill called to this day Bloody Field.

Even at the Passover dinner, the Rabbi of Kálló sang
Hungarian songs, and he compared Jewish slavery in Egypt
to Hungary's bondage to Austria. At his table Gentiles were
welcome—regardless of their status in society. On one occasion, he invited in an old Gentile shepherd, a stranger
covered with rags and smelling of sheep, who appeared at
the door at midnight. To the horror of his other guests—
members of his congregation—the rabbi did nothing to stop
the shepherd from reaching for the cup of the Prophet Elijah,
which is set out at the center of every Passover table in the
pious hope that the legendary wanderer from heaven will
appear and announce the coming of the Messiah. The shepherd drank the wine from Elijah's cup in one gulp, sang a

song at the rabbi's request, and then disappeared, never again to be seen or heard.

The old Gentile shepherd might have been the Prophet Elijah who always travels in disguise, or he was just an old Gentile shepherd. Allowing for the possibility that he was Elijah was risky, even inviting of ridicule, yet the Rabbi of Kálló would not have it otherwise. According to the great authority Yaakov Yitzhak, the Rabbi of Lublin, no one understood the meaning of Passover as profoundly as did Rabbi Taub.

Volumes have been filled with stories about the Rabbi of Kálló, and each story comes in several versions. One common thread is his belief in the healing power of dreams, and another is a ceaseless search to discover the hidden selves of what Jewish mysticism calls "wandering souls"—people whose earlier incarnations were so decisive that they have to find ways to return to them.

In one story I heard many years ago, probably from my grandmother, Rabbi Taub received a visitor from Poland, a Jew sent to him by another rabbi known to perform miracles. The man was a lonely, unhappy soul, and his body, and especially his stomach, was as full of aches as his pocket was full of gold pieces. He could find nothing in life to enjoy. Rabbis and physicians in Poland could not help him and in his desperation, he took the long trip south to Hungary, across the Carpathian mountains, to see the Rabbi of Kálló.

Rabbi Taub listened to the rich man talk about his many problems. Then the rabbi said: "You had a long journey, and you must be tired. It is a beautiful day, a lovely afternoon, so go and rest, and let's hope that your mind will let you fall asleep and that God will send you a good dream." The rabbi

pointed to a large, spreading walnut tree not far from his house
that he thought was a good tree to rest under. It was spring and
the tree had just started leafing out. As soon as the man lay
down under the tree, he fell asleep, and he dreamt.

In his dream the walnut tree was full of leaves, and he
heard a bird singing a beautiful song. He looked up, and on
a branch he saw a bird with golden wings and feet. He called
out, "Come here, bird." The bird flew to the man's shoulder,
and kept on singing.

Suddenly, the bird stopped singing and said, in the voice
of a woman: "Go and visit the doctor who lives next door to
the Rabbi of Kálló. He will cure you."

When the man woke up, the sun was setting. He went to
the synagogue to join the evening prayer. Uncertain about
the importance of the dream, and even more uncertain what
to do about the bird's instructions, he asked the person praying next to him if there was a good doctor in town. He was
told that an excellent physician lived next door to the Rabbi
of Kálló. The man went to see the doctor and told him about
his stomach cramps. The doctor listened and suggested that
he stop eating meat for a few days and see if he might feel
better.

The man did as he was told, and his stomach cramps
disappeared. He went to the synagogue for Shabbos, and he
listened to the Rabbi of Kálló sing. He thought he had never
heard anyone sing so beautifully. He went to see the rabbi,
related the dream, and asked what he should do next. The
rabbi suggested that he might stay in Kálló for another week
and take long walks in the countryside and observe carefully
all there was to see and hear.

In following the rabbi's instructions, the man was surprised to find himself enjoying the sight of meadows and trees. What is more, his body was free of pain. Every day he felt better. The following Shabbos, he went to see the Rabbi of Kálló to thank him and ask what he should do next. The rabbi sent him back to rest under the walnut tree one more time. Again, the man promptly fell asleep and dreamt. In his dream the beautiful bird appeared and sang, then settled on his shoulder and said in the voice of a woman that he should go home to Poland and marry. He would live happily ever after, the bird promised.

The man told the rabbi his dream, and the rabbi advised him to listen to the bird. But before he went home to Poland, the man told his story to the Jews of Kálló, who in turn told the story to others.

In many of the stories collected about the Rabbi of Kálló, he has a faithful companion, a best friend by the name of Aaron Fisch, who was the grandson of Baruch Fisch—the man who saw an angel and who lived one hundred and nineteen years. Aaron Fisch's daughter, Rachel, married Lazar Schwarcz of Derzs, grandson of Daniel, upon whom the Rabbi of Kálló conferred a blessing. And Rachel Fisch was my great-great-grandmother, whose tombstone is still legible in the cemetery of Derzs.

When requested by the Rabbi of Kálló, Aaron Fisch drove him in a carriage to villages often at the far end of Szabolcs County. Aaron Fisch would not ask the purpose of the journey, nor the reason for the timing, which was usually late in the evening, nor why the request always came at short notice. To Aaron Fisch, the journeys seemed to form parts of a quest which he could only dimly understand and which the rabbi only hinted at, using quotes from holy books, such as the one from the mystical Zohar: "A dream uninterpreted is like a letter unread."

On one occasion, when the rabbi was in a particularly agitated state, Aaron Fisch drove him to the village of Levelek, where the rabbi astonished the locals by making inquiries about a young girl answering a certain description. She turned out to be the daughter of a water-carrier, the poorest Jew in the village. The rabbi then proceeded to arrange for a marriage between that girl and a young boy from Poland who grew up in his house.

The rabbi told Aaron Fisch that for years he had searched the villages of Szabolcs County for a girl to marry the boy, an orphan he had been asked to raise many years earlier. The rabbi revealed that in their previous incarnations, the bride and groom had been Roman Catholics and a princess and a prince in Spain. But the fury of the Inquisition and the example of their tutor, who was a secret Jew, turned their souls toward Judaism, and they converted. Joining them in marriage one more time was most important, constituting a miraculous restoration which might hasten the coming of the Messiah.

On another occasion, the Rabbi of Kálló asked Aaron Fisch to go for a ride on the afternoon before the Day of Atonement. With everyone preparing for the meal prior to the fast which began at sunset, it was not a good choice of a time for an outing.

They were riding across land leased by Aaron Fisch when they came upon a small pond he had never seen. Quickly, the Rabbi of Kálló prayed and immersed himself in the water as if it had been a ritual bath. Before his companion could recover from the shock of discovering something as important as a body of water on a piece of property he had worked on for years, the Rabbi of Kálló was dressed and sitting on the wagon next to him.

As soon as the Day of Atonement was over, Aaron Fisch returned to the place he had visited with the Rabbi of Kálló, but he found no body of water, not even a puddle. This time Aaron Fisch could not repress his curiosity. He went to the Rabbi of Kálló and asked for an explanation.

The Rabbi of Kálló said the water they had witnessed was Miriam's Well, which according to Jewish tradition accompanied the children of Israel throughout their years of wandering in the wilderness of Sinai, and which according to Rabbi Taub appeared in Szabolcs County unexpectedly and for only a few hours each time. He gently chided his friend for not taking advantage of an opportunity to immerse himself in a body of pure water to cleanse his body and soul just prior to the Day of Atonement.

The biblical well that the Rabbi of Kálló claimed to have seen resurface in Szabolcs County must have strained the credulity of many a pious Jew. Yet it seems that Aaron Fisch and other ancestors of mine believed the story, which helped shape my family's perception of Hungary, and most particularly of Szabolcs County, as an extension of the Promised Land, if not its surrogate. In her memoirs, my mother writes: "My father had two passions: his family and the fragrant, dark soil of Hungary. His land was his creed, and he instilled that creed in his children."

At my grandfather's funeral, the officiating rabbi was the great-grandson of the Rabbi of Kálló.

The Rabbi of Kálló is also known for having propagated, if not actually composed, an enigmatic song about a miraculous bird that to this day is sung by all Hungarians as a popular folk tune, and by chassidic Jews throughout the

ZÖLD ERDŐBEN, ZÖLD MEZŐBEN

Andantino, ♩ = 63

Nyitra m., K.Z.

Zöld er - dő - ben, zöld me - ző -
Kék a lá - ba, zöld a szár -

ben, zöld er - dő - ben, zöld me - ző - ben
nya, kék a lá - ba, zöld a szár - nya,

la - kik egy ma - dár.
jaj be gyön - gyen jár,

Várj ma - dár, várj, te csak min - dig

várj, még az Is - ten

meg - en - ge - di, ti - ed le - szek már.

m *fi szi l t d' r'*

One version of Rabbi Taub's most famous song about a
wondrous bird, titled "In Green Woods, in a Green Meadow."

world, who sing it in the original Hungarian. It is said that he learned the song from a shepherd.

According to one version of the story, the rabbi heard a young shepherd play the song on his flute, took an instant liking to it and asked the shepherd for the flute. After the rabbi learned to play the melody, he handed back the flute. But the flute, which the shepherd boy had carved out of a walnut branch, could never again play another song, or even produce a sound.

In another version, the composer was the old Gentile shepherd whom the Rabbi of Kálló invited to his Passover table.

The song has a haunting lilt that mixes deep sorrow with exuberant joy. The words are in a code, and the images suggest they might have come from a dream.

The beginning is hopeful: "Dawn is breaking and the cock is crowing. If God so willed it, you could be mine." But this is not a love song, which is made clear by an abrupt switch of theme: "A bird is walking about in a green forest and in a blue meadow." The next line ends with an exclamation point: "What a bird!" What follows is mysterious: "The bird's feet are gold and its wings are gold. The bird is waiting. Wait, bird, wait. Wait, always wait."

Then comes a question that Jews read as a reference to the Messiah: "When will that wait be over?" The answer, missing from the Hungarian version, is the song's one Hebrew line: "When the Temple is rebuilt."

By the time he died, in 1821, Rabbi Taub was Hungary's most celebrated rabbi, a confidant of Jews and Gentiles who went to seek his advice in great numbers. In the year after he died, all Jewish boys born in Szabolcs County were named after him. For nearly twenty years the Jews of Kálló could

Rabbi Taub's crypt today. It was his wish
to be buried next to the highway.

not bring themselves to hire another rabbi and began a new cemetery because they would not allow anyone else to be buried in the cemetery after Rabbi Taub.

In Kálló and in the villages of Szabolcs County, and among descendants of Jews from the eastern part of Hungary, Rabbi Taub is remembered to this day. "The holy rabbi left his footprints in the meadows and the roads he walked through," a day laborer, a churchgoing Roman Catholic tells me. He says he feels privileged to be living across the street from the cemetery where the Rabbi of Kálló lies buried.

His crypt parallels a busy highway and is set back only three feet from the fence. Declining the honor of a center site, usually reserved for rabbis and students of the Talmud, the rabbi asked that his grave be close to the road he enjoyed roaming.

As many as twenty people a day pay their respects and pray at the rabbi's grave. Still others make balls out of the paper on which they have penned their requests and toss them over the six-foot-high concrete wall. The petitions ask for his help to get rid of kidney stones or to obtain a good husband for a daughter who can't find one, to conceive a child or to bring cheer for a man perpetually depressed. The language is Hebrew, Hungarian, or Yiddish, and sometimes a mixture of all three. Some letters read like prayers, others are in a chatty, familiar style, calling him Dear Old Friend, the writers introducing themselves as descendants of members of his congregation, and sharing problems or simply asking to be remembered.

The wind blows, and the papers, many of them pages torn out from spiral notebooks the size of a human hand, fly about. Some are caught by the thorns of tall thistles, and the writing is smudged by rain; other slips find a way in between the weeds and slice into the soft sand.

Looking like a simple peasant house of the nineteenth century, the crypt, made of brick covered with mortar, is crowned with an arching baroque facade, common to the churches and railroad stations built at the time. The outside is painted in the universal yellow of the Habsburg empire that is a bit too bright at first but fades well. Behind the heavy, rusting iron door is a tiny vestibule, and then three steps lead down into a small, low-ceilinged vaulted room without windows that gives the visitor a sensation of being inside a grave. Petitions are everywhere. Folded tight, pieces of paper are stuck into crevices of the crumbling plaster walls and the cracks around the doorframe; they are scattered over the dirt floor and the simple tin tray that is on top of the grave. Hundreds of them are stuffed into a sack, the kind used for grains of wheat, that stands in a corner behind the grave.

In his coffin of unplaned pine, the rabbi dreams his eternal last dream.

Sketches of Jewish characters from nineteenth century Hungarian plays: a pelt merchant on the left and an innkeeper on the right. (Courtesy of the Fettman Chair, Hebrew University, Jerusalem)

4.

Two Barrels of Wine

How much better is your love than wine.
THE BIBLE, SONG OF SOLOMON 1:2

My uncle Shumi—Samuel on his birth certificate—
was meant to be the family chronicler.

As the eldest son, at age twenty-one Shumi complied with the letter of the Jewish law by saying Kaddish for
his father in the synagogue of their village Gyulaj. But he
would not think of sitting where his father sat, the seat of
honor befitting the principal landowner in the village and a
devout Jew. A rationalist, Shumi rejected the piety of his
elders as irrelevant in the twentieth century.

In his waning years, however, Shumi found himself the
last of his generation who both remembered and treasured
the world they had been born into. He decided it was his
mission to track down and maintain contact with relatives
close as well as distant, and to trade with them information
about the lives and thoughts of our family, now scattered
across three continents. Remorseful that he had been an
unsatisfactory son and, as a man without a child of his own,
devoted to his nephews and nieces, he was a most faithful
keeper of our memories.

In 1966, following his sixty-seventh birthday on February
26, he started to commit to writing the family stories he had

been collecting and telling in the last third of his life. He gathered all the details he and other elderly relatives remembered, and he copied all the documents he could find. Pounding with two fingers on his battered portable typewriter from the early 1930s, he filled some one hundred pages—from margin to margin and single-spaced. He did not feel a need for a draft, yet he seldom had to strike over a word or even a letter.

By the end of the year he completed the assignment he had given himself. He dedicated his work to his father and addressed it to me, in the expectation that I would appreciate the stories as much as he did.

His manuscript was not intended for publication, but to be kept in a folder for the benefit of my children he hoped would soon arrive. He said he knew—he argued that it was "only rational"—that one day I would make use of his work in a book.

The following story is a translation of a chapter in his memoirs. Its hero is Shumi's grandfather, who died four years before Shumi was born and with whom Shumi felt a deeper kinship than with his own father, whom he admired but whose footsteps he would not—and could not—follow.

From the wall of the dining room of our home in Gyulaj, a man with a serious face and a well-trimmed beard observes the multitude of his noisy, swarming grandchildren. He seems to be in his sixties or seventies, and he is leaning against a table with one hand. He is my paternal grandfather, Samuel, after whom I was named.

Between this scene and the story I am about to tell, there is a gap of some fifty to sixty years. When I was looking at my grandfather's picture, it must have been in the first years of the twentieth century, and when he left his parents' house in Derzs [a village four miles from Gyulaj] on that wine-buying trip, it must have been in the early 1850s.

Those who lived in the house in Derzs in the period immediately following the defeat of the 1848 revolution must have been going through a turbulent time politically and a harsh period economically. The twenty-acre plot owned by the family and the additional lands they rented did not provide enough for all the needs of a large household and the relatives and guests who passed through. Lazar, the head of the family, worked hard and was on the lookout for money-making ideas during the day, and he spent his nights pondering how to improve his situation.

One day a traveller coming from the highlands of Hungary mentioned that in Bereg County, many miles to the north, there were plenty of good wines maturing in the cellars and they could be obtained at a reasonable price.

That is how the idea came about: somebody must travel to Bereg County, to the village of Drágabártfalva, where lived a righteous and prosperous Jew by the name of Jacob Wiesner, and the wine should be purchased either from him, or with his help, then brought home to Derzs and sold at a decent profit. The head of the family decided that it would be best to send his still-unmarried son, Samuel.

But even before any preparations could be made for the trip, long negotiations had to begin with an honest villager from Derzs, whose reliability was well known but whose horses also had to be inspected and their reliability attested to by the entire village. The mistress of the house started packing for the trip. Who would know today what kinds of provisions were covered under the folk tales' customary description of "biscuits baked in the ashes of a fire"?

The mother had another concern. "Our son does not have the right clothing for such a long journey," she burst out. The head of the family, as modest and undemanding as he was, had to acknowledge that his wife was right. Going to the tailor to have a suit made was out of the question. Then someone suggested that maybe a suit might be borrowed. Fortunately, there was a young villager of similar size and age who gladly contributed to the expedition by lending his suit, somewhat less worn than Samuel's.

Now money had to be found for the purchase of the wine. I don't believe the family had enough money hidden under a mattress, and it is even less likely that they went to a bank. But from somewhere, they managed to put together the necessary amount. Next, they had to acquire two large barrels, clean them thoroughly, treat them with sulfur, and whittle new stoppers for them.

The last order of business was completed one dark night: in great secrecy, someone had to get hold of one of the four carriage rods that reined in the two horses. Because no matter how honest the wagon-owner, nor how much confidence was placed in him as Samuel's companion, it was not necessary for him to know which of the rods had been hollowed-out and stopped up to conceal the money in case the travellers were attacked by robbers.

Now there was really nothing else left to do but for the wagon-owner to go to confession and ask for his priest's blessing. My grandfather visited with the nearest rabbi, who prayed for him and made sure that his package did not lack a protective amulet. At the dawn of a fine day, the wagon rolled out for the big journey.

In those days, it was indeed very long. Now we smile at the distance between the two villages: about seventy miles.

But at that time, it was no small matter to undertake such a journey on bad roads, in uncertainty, in fear of getting lost and of being attacked, and exposed to a thousand dangers.

Crossing the river Tisza at Csap [nowadays the border between Hungary and the Soviet Union] and then leaving behind the town of Ungvár [now part of the Ukraine and called Uzhgorod in Russian], the two travellers reached a mountainous county unfamiliar to them and the horses. Here and there, in small mountain villages, they were given shelter by God-fearing Jews, and the horses could feed on the grass that grew by the roadside. It was not easy to inquire for directions because the local villagers spoke another language, Ruthenian [a dialect of Russian].

At last the travellers sighted the church spire of Drágabártfalva. My grandfather must have stopped the wagon by a brook where he washed himself, straightened out his clothing, cleaned his boots, combed his beard, and chanted the prayer appropriate for the occasion.

Entering the village, they found out where a Jew by the name of Jacob Wiesner lived, and my grandfather, all spruced-up and self-confident, knocked on his door. The man who opened the door was glad to see the travellers because in those days every guest was welcome and appreciated for bringing news about the world outside the village. Besides, the Jewish tradition of hospitality called for a warm reception.

Before my grandfather stepped over the threshold, he did not neglect to kiss the mezuzah on the doorpost. Then came an argument over who should follow whom inside the house, and the travellers insisted that they follow Jacob Wiesner, who was older than either of them. The mistress of the house was also glad to see them and she promptly set the table. Soon there was steaming soup and the smell of meats in a pot wafted their way. A good loaf of challah bread and a bottle of fine kosher wine appeared on the table. After they washed their hands, they sat down. Only during the meal did my grandfather finally have a chance to introduce himself and his companion, and to explain the purpose of his trip from the lowland to the highland.

Jacob Wiesner hastened to assure his guest that he would be helpful in every respect, and his wife suggested that until he completed his business, my grandfather and his companion could stay and eat in their modest house.

The friendly conversation following the meal was interrupted by an unexpected incident. A door opened and in came a young woman, with her long, golden hair untied. She was surprised by the presence of two strange men and promptly ran out. In those days, a woman not putting her hair up and not having a kerchief on her head was as indecent as someone only partially dressed.

My grandfather must have stopped in the middle of a sentence at the sight of the young woman. His wide-open eyes stared in wonder at the handle of the door that closed behind her. He was enchanted.

The father probably mumbled something to the effect that this was his daughter Taube, but the mother must have said: "Oh, what a shameless girl!" Only my grandfather was silent, but not for long.

"Reb Wiesner," he said [using the respectful Yiddish term for master]. "Permit me to ask for your daughter's hand in marriage. I know that you don't know me, but I will tell you everything about myself. My father owns his own land, and he rents additional lands around the village of Derzs, in Szabolcs County. I am twenty-five years old and I don't yet have my own profession. I don't own anything, and even the suit you see on me is borrowed. But I pledge to you that if your beautiful daughter—who should live long and be healthy—becomes my wife, I will make her happy, and she will have many successful children, and I will provide well for them."

I believe that this proposal, made more than a hundred years ago, would surprise even modern parents. It must have taken the Wiesners' breath away and they had to search for the right words to answer, words that would say neither a definite yes or no, words that would neither offend, nor hurt, words that would neither promise nor flatter. After all, daughters were to be given away in marriage, and the young man they faced had courage and was candid and straightforward. However, what sort of a family did he come from, and, oh my God, how far from them would their beloved daughter be living? What could be said?

The wise and down-to-earth Jacob Wiesner knew exactly.

"Son," he began, "first of all, you are tired. You have to spend a few days with us and stay through the Sabbath. I will introduce you to my daughter, and we'll have to hear her opinion too—though that won't decide the matter. In the meantime, you will go ahead and take care of your business, and I will help you there. Then, with God's help, with luck, and with His blessings, you will go home. Then later, after the High Holy Days, if my time permits, I will travel to Derzs, meet your parents—may they live one hundred and twenty years—and take a look at their house and lands. I will discuss with them the issues one usually discusses on such occasions. And, God willing, if I am not disappointed in my expectations—and if my Taube is not more hesitant than what is appropriate—then by spring we can have the wedding.

"But I must warn you that you should not get upset if for

81

example my rabbi advises differently, or if my Taube cries more than what is expected of her, or if my wife cannot reconcile herself to letting our daughter move so far away. Still, I must put your mind at ease that with your open and honest approach, you have already won over my heart, and I hope that I will not be disappointed in my judgment."

In the events that followed, Jacob Wiesner's judgment proved to be right.

My grandfather returned home with an overflowing heart, and with two barrels of wine purchased at a most reasonable price.

He was astonished how much shorter was the journey home. He was received with much happiness, and after reporting on business, he promptly related the rest of what had happened.

Soon, Jacob Wiesner made his way to Derzs, where he found everything to his satisfaction. Next, my great-grandfather Lazar travelled to Drágabártfalva, and that visit was followed by a wedding that lasted three days and three nights, and later, seven wonderful sons and one excellent daughter.

So ends the chapter by Uncle Shumi, which he titled "The Legend of My Grandfather's Marriage."

Reading in between the lines of Shumi's story—which he had heard many times as a child—one imagines that Lazar did not send his son Samuel to such a distant village without first gathering plenty of intelligence, undoubtedly supplied by some of the visitors to his house. His sources must have included the talkative and knowledgeable itinerant beggars making their rounds among the charitable Jews of the country, including Jacob Wiesner, who earned credit in heaven by inviting visitors of all kinds to their dinner tables, particularly on the Sabbath and other holidays.

Importing good wine to a county which produced mostly thin, sour wines was a sound business proposition, and it promised an important new source of income. Lazar must have been advised that it was a good idea to approach in this matter Jacob Wiesner, a merchant and a man of integrity.

Lazar was equally aware that Jacob Wiesner also happened to be a prosperous Jew ready to provide a sizable dowry with his daughter. Uppermost in Lazar's mind must have been the future of his spirited, impetuous son Samuel, who had volunteered to fight for Hungarian independence in the revolution of 1848 and who was determined to make his own choice for a wife. Since Samuel had passed the age of twenty, that choice was imminent.

Lazar's calculations also included the adventure of a long trip, which he hoped would be capped by a meeting with the lovely Taube. It stands to reason that Lazar's informants had reported on the golden hair and the beauty of Jacob Wiesner's daughter as well as her quick wit and knowledge of the Talmud, rare for a woman in those days.

B'shert, my ancestors must have said at the wedding, fond of this swift hammer-blow of a Yiddish word which means "it was meant to be." But my ancestors also knew that it is no meddling with the intentions of the Almighty when someone prepares the ground so that His will may prevail.

5.

A Nobleman Asks for a Favor

The son is born so that he may bear witness to his father's father. . . . Above the darkness of the future burns the star-strewn heaven of the promise: "So shall thy seed be."
FRANZ ROSENZWEIG, *The Star of Redemption*

In the middle of the night, with claps of thunder rolling down from the Carpathian mountains and a rainstorm lashing the windows, my great-grandfather Samuel Schwarcz was awakened by a servant who said that a neighboring landowner had sent an important message that could not wait. Samuel Schwarcz got out of bed.

Standing stock-still outside the bedroom door was a fierce-looking old warrior in a threadbare soldier's tunic that had once been scarlet. He introduced himself as the head servant of a nobleman who lived in a village some fifteen miles away. "My master is asking that you come to see him right now," he said, then clicked his heels and saluted. "He needs you right now," he added.

The request sounded like an order.

Samuel Schwarcz was puzzled. The nobleman, in his seventies, was a few years his senior, and the one time they had met was nearly a half a century before and then only briefly. The last in Szabolcs County to bear the name of an old and famous family of military officers and government officials, the nobleman had a reputation as a recluse and eccentric. A lifelong bachelor, he had shocked the county the previous

A contemporary engraving shows Lajos Kossuth, leader of Hungary's 1848 rebellion against the imperial Habsburg regime, addressing a crowd.

year by marrying an eighteen-year-old peasant girl from a village where he owned most of the land and where all the peasants worked for him—just as the peasants' ancestors had worked as serfs for his noble ancestors for centuries preceding the liberation of serfs in 1848. It was said that the girl was neither pretty nor plain, neither smart nor stupid. She was just a poor, ordinary peasant who could never think of going beyond the four grades of the village school.

The thought of delaying an answer didn't even occur to Samuel Schwarcz. Not only was the man who sent for him a member of the feudal upper class whose word was still the law, but Samuel Schwarcz was not the kind of person who refused a neighbor's appeal for help.

He looked at the servant's wizened face, as immobile and inscrutable as a reptile's, and he knew that it would be useless to try to pry out of him a word of explanation. He dressed quickly and climbed into the carriage—a battered, creaky black stagecoach—the nobleman had sent for him. The old warrior, who also served his master as coachman, cursed the entire way as he tried, without much success, to force his two lean nags into a gallop.

Samuel Schwarcz too was eager to get to the nobleman's village. Weighing the possibilities that might have prompted the strange invitation kept him awake. A need for a loan? Not in the middle of the night. A wish to sell some land? Not in a storm. A deathbed confession or last wish? They were not friends. A Jew in trouble in the nobleman's village? The nobleman was not known as a friend of the Jews. Samuel Schwarcz's lively mind could not produce a single plausible explanation.

When they finally arrived in the village, the nobleman was

waiting outside, by the gate to his house, oblivious to the rain.

"I have a son," the nobleman announced gravely as he shook his guest's hand. "He was born a few hours ago, prematurely, and I am worried about him. He is small and puny, and whatever the doctor says, to me he looks like a person who will not be on this earth for very long. I want you to say the appropriate prayer for him, in your language and according to your custom, so he may live. Then I want you to be the first person to kiss him."

Samuel Schwarcz did not understand. Why on earth should a Roman Catholic want an old Jew to be the first person to kiss his son, and pray for his health too, as if he were a Jewish child? But he did as he was told, asked no questions, and waited patiently for an explanation.

"Tomorrow morning, when he will be christened, I will name my son Samuel—after you," the nobleman said as he escorted his guest from the nursery, which was cluttered with broken-down chairs and sagging bookcases jammed with books and papers, to a spacious, high-ceilinged parlor dominated by a huge leather-covered sofa and two matching armchairs. The leather was the color of withered leaves, and horsehair stuck out in tufts where the creases had worn through. The chairs' armrests ended in carved lions' heads and the legs were in the shape of lions' paws.

Tall, thick candles in wrought iron stands were already lit, and their light deepened the pallor of the nobleman's skin, which was as gray as ashes and as thin as parchment. But his dark eyes, framed by dark eyelashes, were like live coals.

An old woman entered, carrying a silver tray with a bottle of plum brandy, two silver cups, and some cakes. She bowed to both men and told Samuel Schwarcz that she was Jewish and lived in the nobleman's village and that he had asked her to provide kosher food and drink.

Samuel Schwarcz thanked his host for his thoughtfulness and proposed a toast to the newborn's health and happiness. The nobleman muttered an uncertain and soft "amen" to the Jew's firm and loud "l'chaim."

While Samuel Schwarcz downed the contents of his glass in one lusty gulp, the nobleman took only a cautious sip.

"I see that you drink like a true son of Szabolcs County," the nobleman said.

"It's what the doctor orders to settle the stomach and to lift the spirit," his guest replied.

But that was the end of small talk. The nobleman didn't waste time in getting to his point.

"I want you and your sons to look after my son after I am gone," he said. "When I die, my relatives—who do not even bear my family's name—will want to prove that I was too old to sire an heir. They will band together and make use of their many connections in high places to try to take away my land from my son. I know I can rely on you to fight for my son's lawful inheritance.

"I will name you my executor, Samuel Schwarcz. I want you to keep my son here, in this old house and on this ancestral land. You will make sure that he does not sell any of the estate. It is six hundred acres of reasonably good land, though it does need the attention of a well-trained, modern agronomist. I never had an interest in farming, but I want you to make sure—and I rely on you, a successful father of eight children, to choose whatever methods of persuasion you find appropriate—that my son will become a model steward of the land like you, and not an absentee landowner squandering his wealth, playing cards, attending the theater, and chasing women in Budapest and Vienna."

Samuel Schwarcz nodded, more in embarrassment than in agreement, and his face reflected his confusion. But when he tried to ask a question, the nobleman interrupted him.

"I know that you agree with me that the land is the only reality that truly matters and is worth living and dying for, rather than such lofty illusions as motherland or empire," he said. "I also think that you will agree with me that those illusions are created by people prompted by their own madness or self-interest, and they can only lead the rest of us astray."

The nobleman scorned "the supreme folly of the 1848 revolution," which he called "a feast of the national vice of dreaming while awake." Reason would have called for "an orderly, gradual improvement of the lot of the serfs" and "a calm, measured reconciliation with our more advanced, more civilized Austrian neighbor." But he was scathing in condemning "the treasonous ease" and "abject haste" with which Hungarians made peace with Emperor Franz Josef less than twenty years after his forces crushed the revolution and wreaked bloody vengeance on its leaders.

"Franz Josef's hands were stained with the blood of our people," he intoned. "We should not have forgiven him so easily. Ours is a nation of daydreamers who whine and grovel after they realize that their daydreams do not get them anywhere. Every Hungarian lives for the fine mist of an evening spent drinking wine when after a few glasses each outrageous idea that pleases him for the moment seems to him not only possible but within his reach. He does not think of the hangover that comes in the morning.

"One neighbor of mine dreams of an estate of hundreds of

acres which he claims the law took away from his ancestors by mistake two centuries ago, but which he hopes to win back on the basis of documents he will uncover one day in the county archives or someone's trunk. In the meantime he barely has enough to eat. Another fine citizen of this great county of ours believes that our national poet, Sándor Petöfi, was not killed on the battlefield by the Russians in 1849 but taken to Siberia as a prisoner of war, and that he returned to Hungary in disguise and visited him some years ago. He is still looking for the poet who keeps talking to him in his dreams. He writes letters to people throughout the country who also claimed to have sighted the poet. He does nothing else and lives off his inheritance.

"I may be the only sober man left in this county, and I want to bury this dream-inundated century of ours and our entire drunken past."

The nobleman was certain that the twentieth century, only a few years away, would finally shatter the obsolete alliances formed by class, religion, and nationality. It would be a century of justice, enlightenment, and equality, he predicted. Classes would be abolished, and empires and nation-states, restless minorities and proud military castes would all bow to the authority of a supremely rational world government.

He warned Samuel Schwarcz to be prepared to accept the inevitable: that his grandchildren would shave off their beards, marry Gentiles, and stop keeping kosher. Churches and synagogues alike would be empty. In their misery, priests and rabbis would seek out one another and make friends.

Samuel Schwarcz listened. Early on he realized that he was not expected to speak. As he hung on to his host's words, his lively brown eyes and mobile eyebrows reflected both sympathy and skepticism. But neither reaction seemed to matter to the nobleman, who was bent on delivering his monologue.

"I am an anachronism," he declared. "I am living off ghosts who live with me in this house. I believe in reason and rationality, and I keep telling the people in my village that there are no ghosts, the dead are dead, and those alive are alive, and there can be no traffic between the two. Yet I hear ghosts, and they are my poor unhappy ancestors muttering curses at kings and fellow knights long dead. They never have a good word for anybody.

I myself am a ghost. I own this land because nearly a millennium ago a king was pleased by something done by a forefather of mine. Or maybe it was a woman ancestor. God only knows how it really happened that my family joined the ranks of the nobility and became so famous and powerful.

"But can there be any reason in the world to own such a large piece of land when so many peasants own no land at all? What right do I have to make the peasants work for me, to have them sweat and toil to earn my living? Is privilege forever?

"It is good that my son has peasant blood on his mother's side. It is the peasants working on the land who really own it."

The nobleman finally turned to the subject of the Jews.

"I am not a modern man," he said. "I have never befriended a Jew. They are too intense, too eager, too ambitious. But I don't dislike them, and I dislike those who dislike Jews.

"I am afraid of Jews. I cannot help it: I reflect the centuries that have passed. But I also know that my world—the unjust old world based on the absurd whims of royalty and the gross privileges of nobility—is dying. Some of my fellow noblemen try to keep it alive by invoking their merits: their historical leadership in the conquest of Hungary a thousand years ago and their role in organizing the armies fighting off foreign invasions in the centuries that followed. What rubbish! What hypocrisy! Hungarian nobility hasn't fought a war for centuries! It is no longer a military caste—if it was ever really that.

"I don't want to resurrect the old world. Let it die and let it be buried deep in the earth, as it must, and the sooner the funeral the better! In the new world that is being born, peasants with their strength and Jews with their brains will play the leading roles. We, the nobility, can no longer keep down the peasants and the Jews, and whatever mistakes I made in my life, I am proud that I have never wanted to exclude the peasants or the Jews.

"There is a strange tradition in my family going back many generations: when we are in trouble, we turn to a Jew. I chose you because you and your family believe in the land the way I do.

"You buy costly new equipment from abroad, you try to enrich this thin, sandy soil we are cursed with. You experiment. You keep buying land, no matter how poor it is or where it is. I may be a hermit but I have a fairly good idea how much you must have paid to bribe the government surveyors and engineers to drain the swamps near your properties."

The nobleman ignored his guest, who had raised his hand as if he were a student in school.

"I am not a moralist," the nobleman continued. "I don't sit in judgment over you or anyone else. What you did was right for the land. I don't give a damn about what people might think.

"I am a writer. Many years ago I started writing a philosophical treatise about the hidden meaning of Hungarian history. I wanted to explain why we are different from all the other nations in Europe: because we are Asian nomads who married the sedentary Slavs we found in this land and because this land has been a Promised Land absorbing not just conquerors but waves of immigrants. I abandoned that project. For some years I have been working on a novel to summarize all that I have seen in my long and pointless life.

"Every night I write. I work until daybreak, then I go to sleep. I don't like the sunlight, and I don't want to meet people. I wake up in the afternoon, and around sunset I read what I wrote the night before. I hate it. The words never say what I want to say. So I burn all the pages in the fireplace.

"I have divested myself of ideologies, of allegiances to beliefs and 'isms.' I have also become an atheist. I no longer carry the burden of any great cause. I am a free man!"

Samuel shook his head in disapproval. A hint of a smile flickered across the nobleman's face as he continued.

"The piety of Jews baffles me. I can see how Roman Catholics and Calvinists benefit from their faith. But how can you keep believing in your Yahweh of the wilderness when it is clear that he abandoned you ages ago? How can you ignore the persecution and the ridicule of the world and keep following all those hundreds of rules and restrictions that Moses said Yahweh wanted you to follow? Your daydream makes your life difficult. Your allegiance is to an abstraction. Your faith in the Messiah is absurd. Despite all your subtle intelligence and smart planning, you are one of life's fools, Samuel Schwarcz. But that's why I trust you."

Samuel Schwarcz did not understand everything the nobleman said. ("Why does his family turn to Jews only when they are in trouble?" he later asked his wife Taube. "And

how did such a tradition start?" "And why do we Jews take
up the burden?" Taube replied.) But he accepted the trust.
("What else could I do?" he said to Taube, shrugging, his
hands up in the air. "What else could any man with feelings
do?" "You are right," Taube said. "But the nobleman was
smart enough to turn to the right Jew.")

The truth that Samuel Schwarcz was embarrassed to tell
his wife was that as he sat in a peeling leather armchair in
the nobleman's ramshackle mansion that had not been painted
for decades, he felt rewarded. It was as if he had been dec-
orated for valor and meritorious service. In his hour of crisis,
a neighbor turned to him and chose him from among all the
people in the county. He, Samuel Schwarcz, became the
confidant of a lonely, noble soul in distress, and he was
entrusted with what was most precious to that soul: a son and
an heir to the family land. He was to ensure that a puny
newborn would play a role that had been preordained. He
thought of the blessing his own family had received. As the
image of the Rabbi of Kálló laying his hands over Great-
grandfather Daniel's head and promising success on the land
passed through his mind, Samuel Schwarcz's lips remembered
the softness of the baby's face he had kissed, and he felt
moved when he thought of the father's loyalty to his son and
his land.

Throughout that long night, Samuel Schwarcz could not
help seeing in the frail, bent figure of the nobleman a tall,
ramrod-straight lieutenant in a scarlet hussar's uniform who
had come to his native village of Derzs in that faraway, unforgettable spring of 1848 and made an eloquent speech in
front of the Calvinist church. The lieutenant called for vol-
unteers to fight for the revolution's aims of independence from
Austria, union with Transylvania, the abolition of censorship,

and a democratically elected parliament accountable to the people. He pledged that the revolutionary army would crush tyranny, end all oppression, and bring about a new world of equality.

Samuel was eighteen then, unmarried, and built more like a stocky peasant than like a student in the cheder, the traditional Jewish school. In a daze, he had walked over to the lieutenant, shaken his hand, and signed up to join the army.

Even if the nobleman did not remember that handshake, so critical to the recruit, he must have known that Samuel Schwarcz had fought in the revolutionary war. In Szabolcs County, always a center of patriotic fervor, people kept mental files on what everyone did in the all-important time of 1848–49. However, the nobleman made no mention of that shared moment of glory in their youth, and Samuel Schwarcz did not have a chance to raise the subject.

Dawn was breaking when the host suggested that his guest might be tired. The nobleman walked the Jew to the carriage that was ready to go, the horses harnessed, and the coachman sitting stiffly on his seat.

The rain had stopped some time before, and a thick fog covered the land like a coarse woolen blanket.

On the way home, Samuel Schwarcz did not feel a bit tired. He thought of lawyers and depositions, equipment to be bought and men to be hired. Six hundred acres was a lot of land, and with improvements and good management, the property would produce real wealth. That little fellow he accepted responsibility for had a brilliant future.

Samuel Schwarcz never saw the nobleman again. In the months that followed, as the son gathered strength, the father grew weaker and died before the child's first birthday.

Old Samuel did not forget young Samuel. The will was contested, as predicted, but Samuel Schwarcz found a good lawyer, arranged for witnesses, reassured the frightened widow, and made sure that nothing came of the lawsuit. There were hard business decisions for the inexperienced and ignorant widow, but Samuel Schwarcz was there to help.

When Samuel Schwarcz died, at the threshold of the twentieth century, little Samuel attended the funeral. With an unaccustomed skullcap pinned to his flaxen hair, he stood with old Samuel's eight children, holding the hand of the one daughter, and he wept along with them. They were all adults, and one of them promised to look after him.

Little Samuel grew up to be good-natured, straightforward, generous, a strapping peasant lad with hands as large as shovels. He studied agronomy, and when he returned home, he worked hard and raised the value of his estate little by little.

When the First World War broke out in 1914, he was drafted and given the rank of second lieutenant—after all, his father had been a nobleman and an officer. Dispatched to fight what the popular song called "the dog Serbs who murdered the Archduke," he was among the first to fall in what the official notification termed "the field of honor."

Young Samuel left no child. But there were plenty of debts to pay off and mortgages to renegotiate. Within a year, the estate had to be auctioned off. Influential relatives bought most of the ancestral land; Samuel's mother was able to keep the mansion. She was, however, beyond consolation. When she had become a widow, she always dressed in layers of black like an old peasant woman. After her son's death, everyone understood why she could not stay sober for one evening.

The Schwarcz estate was in trouble too. Several of Samuel's children had bought too much land and could not pay all the mortgages. They had taken far too many risks, for the Schwarcz faith in improvement and progress was boundless.

The price of wheat plummeted, and war bonds, oversubscribed for patriotic reasons, could not be redeemed because the Austro-Hungarian monarchy lost the war and fragmented into many parts. A Romanian occupation of the eastern part of Hungary and a communist coup d'etat in Budapest produced a chaos that was worse than the war, and waves of looters in and out of uniform swept through the countryside. Roving bands of soldiers returning from the front and from prisoner-of-war camps ravaged estates large and small, carting away and destroying equipment, stealing horses and cattle, and setting barns on fire.

The alliances which linked the great monarchies of the Old World turned out to serve as a suicide pact for the Habsburgs, the Hohenzollerns, the Romanoffs, and the Ottomans. When order was finally restored in Hungary, and an admiral from the monarchy's navy took over the land-locked kingdom as its regent, the Schwarcz brothers and their children had conflicting ideas on how to save their ancestral domain. A few years after peace was signed in Versailles, the family cemetery—the first plot of land acquired God knows how many centuries earlier—was the only land left from Samuel Schwarcz's inheritance that was still registered in the Schwarcz name.

My grandparents Róza and Karl Schwarcz in 1896, shortly after they got married.

6.

The True Rachel

A woman of valor who can find?
For her price is far above rubies.
THE BIBLE, PROVERBS 31:10

O nce upon a time, in the early 1890s, when the white-
bearded Emperor Franz Josef kept the peace among
his Austrians and Hungarians, Poles and Romanians,
Catholics and Protestants, Jews and Moslems, a wedding was
held in the little town of Nagykároly in Transylvania, then in
Hungary, and now called Karei, in Romania. Underneath a
velvet canopy embroidered with silk threads of purple and
gold, and in accordance with the laws of Moses, a slender
young man by the name of Zhigmond, a wealthy owner of
wheatfields, cattle, and sheep, took as his wife a lovely young
woman by the name of Sarah, the older of the two daughters
of a respected local banker by the name of Kaufmann.

The groom's brothers, including one younger by the Hebrew
name of Akiba, who according to custom was to marry next,
were introduced to the bride's younger sister, also unmarried
and uncommonly beautiful, whose Hebrew name was Rachel.
After exchanging a few polite words—the maximum contact
permitted by the custom of the time—Akiba's heart was cap-
tured. Moreover, he had the impression, nothing more and
nothing less than an impression but an impression nonetheless, that Rachel looked at him with favor.

As soon as the wedding dinner was over, Akiba took aside his favorite brother Yankev and prevailed upon him to approach Rachel's father and explore gingerly what his reaction might be to the idea of a second alliance between the two families.

"Such a match is simply out of the question," was the banker's prompt and blunt response to Yankev. "I have two daughters, and I don't want to see them married to two brothers—and particularly not when both of them are engaged in agriculture. I don't want to argue any more with your father—may he live to the fullness of days—that owning and cultivating land is a wholesome business and the best way to make a living. Your brother is now my son-in-law, and that means that I don't reject your family philosophy.

"But when making investments, it is never wise to put all of one's assets in one type of enterprise. Prudence suggests that my daughter Rachel marry someone active in industry or commerce, or perhaps medicine or the law."

Yankev was dismissed.

The two brothers went for a walk to discuss what to do next. Yankev thought that the banker's objection was too strong and visceral, and suggested that in the days to come Akiba should reexamine the certainty of his attraction to Rachel. Yankev's advice was not to argue the point any more, at least for the moment—and certainly not to mention it to their parents. As usual, Akiba listened to his brother.

Akiba returned to his father's house and did his best to try to forget Rachel Kaufmann. Yankev went home to his village with his wife.

The wedding in Nagykároly had been held on Lag b'Omer, the lighthearted spring holiday of picnics and bonfires. Lag b'Omer is considered auspicious for the celebration of marriage—a new beginning—because it was on that day that Shimon bar Yochai, the great talmudic sage and mystic, was ordained as a rabbi, and it was on that same day that he emerged from the cave where he had hidden from the Romans who sought to arrest and execute him.

Next on the calendar, at the edge of summer, was the joyous harvest festival of Shavuos. It is said that the heavens open during the night of Shavuos and that the Almighty is more likely to respond to a mortal's plea than at any other time of the year. Akiba prayed for help to forget Rachel Kaufmann.

Then came Tisha b'Av, the fast day to remember the searingly hot summer day on which the Romans, and before them the Babylonians, set fire to the Temple in Jerusalem. Akiba prayed while sitting on the ground barefoot and shed tears for the Temple and for the Jewish people exiled from the Holy Land, and for himself as well.

Soon, it was Rosh Hashanah, the beginning of a new year. The wheat harvest was in, sheep grew their thick winter fleece, and the rains of autumn began. But Akiba did not feel renewed.

On Yom Kippur, the day when a Jew reviews the events of the year that passed and takes stock of his life, Akiba concluded that he could not banish Rachel Kaufmann's face from his mind. He kept his thoughts to himself.

At Simchas Torah, the celebration of the Five Books of Moses, Akiba danced around the Torah scroll and sang like everyone else, but he did not feel the burst of energy the holiday had always given him.

Winter came, and the long evenings drew Akiba deeper

and deeper into melancholy. He paid no attention to his brothers, who kept reporting to him the proposals for Akiba that the matchmaker brought to their parents.

It was during Purim, the festival of spring fever, that the parents decided they must find out what had happened to the usually cheerful Akiba. He sat by himself, quietly, while everyone drank wine, loudly cursed the tyrant Haman who had sought to kill all the Jews of Persia, and cheered the brilliant and beautiful Esther who had brought down Haman and saved her fellow Jews.

The parents extracted a confession from Yankev who had come home for the holiday and whose tongue was loosened by the wine. The three of them decided that something had to be done immediately and the best thing to do was for Akiba to go to the renowned Rabbi Yissachar Dov and ask for his advice. The rabbi was not only saintly and learned in the Talmud but had a rare reputation as one who "understood the hearts of men." He lived far away, and both a long journey and a change in the landscape were considered helpful in repairing a broken heart. Naturally, Yankev would accompany his brother.

Akiba liked the idea, and in a few days he and Yankev were on their way to the little town of Belz, some three hundred miles to the northeast, on the other side of the snow-covered Carpathian mountains, at the edge of the Habsburg emperor's Polish province of Galitzia and nowadays on the Russian side of the Polish-Russian border. It took more than two weeks for the brothers to travel there in their father's best carriage drawn by a pair of his most surefooted horses. The wind did not stop whipping, and it was colder than they had ever remembered feeling. The brothers shivered in their sheepskin coats.

In the center, wearing a fur hat, is the Rabbi of Belz, Yissachar Dov, who plumbed the depths of the Talmud and understood the hearts of men.

A turn-of-the-century postcard showing the synagogue in Belz, a small town now in the Soviet Union. The Nazis burned the synagogue down.

They were surprised by how much more impoverished Galitzia was than Hungary. They picked up beggars and other travellers who talked about the poor soil and the government oppression, but who said that life was even worse across the border, where the czar ruled.

Belz was not hard to find, the brothers were told, because the golden finials on top of the synagogue glitter for a distance of many miles. The synagogue, which was in the center of the town of nearly 3,000 people, was unlike any other. It looked like a fortress, and was built by the grandfather of the current rabbi who not only designed the square structure—an unusual shape for a synagogue—but took part in the construction himself, spreading mortar and laying bricks with his own hands.

The brothers marvelled at the beauty and harmoniousness of the synagogue and the spaciousness of Rabbi Yissachar Dov's house next to it. The buildings were well heated and filled with petitioners who talked about their previous visits with the rabbi and praised the sage advice they had received. The brothers, who had never before seen the rabbi, waited for their turn, which came past midnight.

The rabbi was tall and robust, and wore trousers and an ankle-length coat with a belt, all made of the same fine, lustrous black cloth that looked like silk. He was old, and his curly white beard covered his shirtfront. His dark eyes sparkled and he looked at the two young men as if he knew exactly why they came to see him. They kissed his hand, and he invited them to sit in two high-backed chairs facing his.

"What is troubling you, my son Akiba?" he asked.

Akiba explained that he had met a beautiful woman by the name of Rachel Kaufmann, younger sister to his brother Zhigmond's wife, Sarah, and that he had fallen in love with her, and even believed that she was not indifferent to him, but that her father, a banker, would not hear of marrying his two daughters to two brothers, both of them engaged in agriculture.

"The banker is a hard-headed businessman, Your Honor," Yankev told the rabbi, "and my brother Akiba has the soft heart of a poet. But they are both stubborn."

The rabbi listened patiently to Akiba's detailed, impassioned account and Yankev's brief commentary. Then he took Akiba's hands and looked into his eyes for a long time and, finally, smiled.

He stroked his beard and said, "Go home in peace, my dear son Akiba, for there is another Rachel Kaufmann waiting for you."

The audience was over. The two brothers left Belz at dawn the following day.

The first few days of the journey home were uneventful. The air was crisp, and the cold felt invigorating. Akiba pondered what the rabbi had said and wondered aloud: did the rabbi hint at some change that may affect Rachel Kaufmann's situation? Might the father change his mind? Or did the rabbi mean that he would eventually meet *another* woman named Rachel Kaufmann? (The name was not uncommon, though not an everyday name either.) Or did the rabbi simply mean that he would meet another fine woman like Rachel Kaufmann—because, Rachel or Leah, Ruth or Devorah, for the old rabbi one young woman was just like any other. Or was there perhaps yet another, hidden meaning in those words that Akiba was destined to uncover?

Yankev said nothing because Akiba said all there was to

say. Yankev thought it would be best not to analyze the rabbi's words too much but simply wait and let events take their course.

The brothers chanted their prayers, and the rest of the time Yankev sang songs, as was his custom. For the first time in many months, Akiba requested that Yankev sing certain songs, and Akiba once again praised Yankev's fine voice, as he had done in the days before Rachel Kaufmann.

Without any warning, a fierce snowstorm tumbled down from the sky and billowed up from the valleys below, blinding man and horse. Snowflakes the size of plums swirled around the carriage. As the brothers tried to make their way along the unfamiliar mountain road, the carriage skidded and slammed into a rock, snapping the axle in two. The brothers mounted the horses and rode for a long time before they reached a village.

Fortunately, there was an inn, which was owned by a Jew. His name was Kaufmann, and he was a talkative, cheerful old man glad to receive visitors from the lowland of Hungary. They talked business as well, and it didn't take long for the innkeeper, who also did some trading, to come up with a proposal. He would supply lumber from his area in exchange for the brothers' wheat and sheep's fleece. As they discussed the details, a young woman walked into the room.

"This is my brother's only daughter, Rachel," said the innkeeper, introducing her. "She is also my one and only niece, now visiting my wife and me. She is like a daughter to us because, unfortunately, the Almighty did not bless us with a child."

Akiba looked at the woman. She was slim, petite, with wavy auburn hair gathered in a chignon. She had a delicate, heart-shaped face, and green eyes. She wore a long blue dress with a lace collar. She was soft and lovely, and Akiba had no doubt she was the Rachel Kaufmann the rabbi had promised.

After the brothers had dinner and retired to the guest room, Akiba asked Yankev to talk to the innkeeper next morning and suggest marriage. "But this time, don't use a tentative approach," Akiba said. "Just be straightforward."

Yankev did as he was told. The innkeeper replied that he was honored by the interest on the part of such a fine young man, but, of course, as he had already made clear, Rachel was not his daughter but his brother's, and in any case, the two young men had better go home and talk to their father first.

The innkeeper helped the brothers find someone in the village to replace the axle, and by midafternoon, with the sun shining, the snow melting, and the scent of spring in the air, the carriage was speeding home.

Akiba's parents were delighted to hear what the rabbi had had to say, and the story of the encounter in the inn brought tears to their eyes. It took the father only a few weeks before he arranged to visit Rachel Kaufmann's parents, who lived in the village of Töketerebes, some seventy miles to the northeast, then still part of Hungary and now in the Soviet Union. He discovered that Rachel Kaufmann's father too owned and leased land, and considered farming the ideal profession. The two fathers liked each other instantly and they came quickly to an agreement about their children.

By Lag b'Omer, in the year 1895, they were married: Akiba, my grandfather, and Rachel, my grandmother.

Grandfather Karl in 1891, when he was thirty.

7.

A Stroll under the
Horse-Chestnut Trees

Dear God! the heart, the very heart of me
That plays and strays, a truant in strange lands,
Always returns and finds its inward peace,
Its swing of truth, its measure of restraint,
Here among meadows, orchards, lanes and shaws.
VITA SACKVILLE-WEST, *Night*

In Vienna, I never walk alone. For company, I have my maternal grandfather, Karl Schwarcz, who died in 1920, shortly after the First World War ended and seventeen years before I was born. As a young man, he attended Vienna's Consular Academy, a liberal institution that trained diplomats and other loyalists for the conservative Habsburg monarchy, and he learned to love the glittering Austrian imperial capital almost as much as the tiny Hungarian village of Derzs, where he had been born in 1861 and its equally modest neighbor, Gyulaj, where he built his house and set up his estate. According to the family legend, he travelled to Vienna nearly every year, and once during each visit he waited for Emperor Franz Josef's carriage to pass in front of the Hofburg Palace. When it came, always on time, he shouted, with his silver-topped walking stick held high, "Long live the King of Hungary!"

On at least one occasion, the king-emperor nodded, acknowledging his subject's demonstration of loyalty. The memory of that nod—always called "a gracious nod"—was carried back to Gyulaj as a souvenir to be treasured and to be cited to family and friends, again and again, from generation to generation.

109

I was named after my grandfather. My Hebrew name, Akiba, and my Hungarian name, Károly—which he used in the German form of Karl and which I translated into Charles when I emigrated to the United States—were both his. Every morning when I shave, I can't help seeing his face in mine. Along with his gold pocket watch, I inherited his ease in straddling cultures and controversies, his attachments to family and land, and his genre of optimism, of a type common to fathers and gardeners.

When my children were born, I recalled the Yiddish saying, "Each child brings its own luck." When I see a plant sprout, I remember the belief that behind each blade of grass stands an angel, whispering, "Grow, dear grass, grow!" I know—I know—that my grandfather thought the same thoughts, thrived on the same traditional formulas, and when I think of how much I echo him, I feel as reassured as if the biblical patriarch Abraham blessed me.

Every time I visit Vienna, I find I must go for a stroll under the horse-chestnut trees which my grandfather was so fond of. Like the Viennese, he admired their towers of dense, deep green foliage, arrayed in tidy double rows. Their shady allées were designed to inspire solitary contemplation as well as to shelter romance. The allée is the forest tamed and yet still the forest, and while my grandfather rooted for civilization and progress, he was for holding on to the primal green as well.

I remember my grandmother Róza remembering how in the fall, when she travelled to Vienna with her husband and they walked under the horse-chestnut trees, he used his walking stick to hit the spiky husks scattered on the ground so they split, releasing the nuts that were shinier than the chestnuts they resembled and as brown as a crust of Hungarian bread.

110

There were always a few horses pulling fiacres to snap up the nuts.

The history of the horse-chestnut tree is a parable on the shifting fortunes of empires and the enduring beauty of plants. Horse-chestnut trees originate on the hillsides of the Balkans, where a conquering Turkish sultan with an esthete's eye discovered their choice greenery and ordered his pashas to plant them along streets and in parks. As the Ottoman crescent began to wane, its nemesis, Prince Eugen of Savoy, the brilliant French general who commanded the Austrian imperial forces, was captivated by the stateliness of the trees. He imported the first saplings to Vienna after his Christians drove the last Moslem Turk out of Hungary in 1699.

The ethereal spires of the tree's white flowers, as tall as twelve inches and rising by the hundreds out of the foliage, are upright and have a solemn symmetry. In the Roman Catholic parts of the Habsburg empire, the flowers were promptly baptized as Candles of the Virgin Mary. Then an Austrian poet whose name even my learned Viennese friends no longer recall decided that the leaf emerged out of the depths of Vienna's baroque soul and was an artistic representation of the human hand. Thus the horse-chestnut tree became Vienna's finest street tree and botanical icon.

In these days of faded glory, Vienna's horse-chestnut allées have an engagingly uneven mixture of old and young trees, and experts assure me that some of them were planted in the first years of this century, and a few even earlier. It occurs to me that, as saplings, today's oldest trees were seen by my grandfather.

Coming from flood plains dominated by the slow-moving Tisza, one of the Danube's many tributaries, my grandfather, travelling by train or carriage, liked to follow the course of the swift Danube winding its way through hills and plains. He thought of the Danube as the thread that stitches together all the lands from Germany to the Black Sea. A Hungarian patriot, he nevertheless found it not inconsistent to believe ardently in the need for a confederation of Danubian states, perhaps under the rule of a thoughtful Habsburg. Then, as now, such a confederation is a pipe dream, unchartered and untimely, a favorite of people of good intentions. It is too impractical an idea for a region of obstreperous nationalities contending with one another and against aggressive empires.

Like so many Hungarians of his generation, Karl Schwarcz admired Franz Josef as the peacemaker of his time. He did so despite the fact that at age eighteen, his father and hero, Samuel, had volunteered in the revolution of 1848 to fight Franz Josef, also eighteen, an impulsive act invariably cited as a justification whenever someone in the family struck out on a risky course.

For my grandfather, Franz Josef personified not only decency and fairness, but also predictability, that much sought-after comfort of middle age as well as the most solid of bourgeois virtues. (Unpredictability is the tyrant's pleasure; his subjects compete in analyzing his caprice, and he exults in the fact that only he and no one else knows where and whom he will strike next.) Predictability was seldom as widely appreciated as in Franz Josef's era, in which the growing and prospering bourgeoisie believed in continuing growth and prosperity. To his nearly fifty million subjects, Franz Josef offered the best years of peace and the fairest system of justice his part of the world had known then or since. For the generation that grew old and rich with him, longevity and prosperity appeared as if they had been gestures of loyalty to him.

In one respect, Franz Josef was most unlike the bourgeoisie. In a culture devoted to comfort, he was a puritan who slept on a narrow, steel-framed army cot, rose at five o'clock every morning and retired at nine—or ten if a state dinner kept him up. He ate little, and his one indulgence was a baby biscuit called ladyfingers which he dipped in champagne. Dyspeptic and unhappy, he was a prisoner of convention and caution, the Austro-Hungarian monarchy's number one civil servant, dedicated to paperwork and parades, inaugurations and inspections. He was a most dutiful emperor, as reliable as the mechanical knight of a clock tower.

With every year, my grandfather grew fonder of the Old Emperor. When he heard the news of Franz Josef's death, on a grim November day in 1916, he sat down at his rolltop desk, cradled his face in his hands, and wept. He ordered that a huge black banner, two pieces of black fabric six yards long, stitched together side by side and nailed to a sturdy pole, be hung from the roof.

It was as if the clock had stopped ticking, as if time had come to a halt.

As a child, I listened to Uncle Shumi telling me the story of Franz Josef's burial according to the medieval rite of the Habsburgs. After the requiem mass at St. Stephen's Cathedral, the long imperial cortege moved through the streets of Vienna at a slow pace. Finally, it arrived in front of the Church of the Capuchin Friars, the burial place of the Habsburgs. But the chamberlain leading the procession was surprised to find the doors closed. He knocked.

Who is there? came the question from within the church.

The chamberlain said he was demanding entrance to the imperial vault for His Imperial Majesty Franz Josef I, Emperor of Austria and Apostolic King of Hungary, King of Bohemia, Dalmatia, Croatia, Slavonia, Galitzia, Lodomeria, and Illyria. In a loud voice, the chamberlain listed all the many titles Franz Josef had acquired.

There is no room left here, boomed the anonymous voice from within the church.

Angry, the chamberlain banged on the door and demanded that it be opened forthwith, in the name of the emperor.

There was no answer from within, and an awkward silence descended on the mourners standing outside.

Then, in a low voice, the chamberlain asked if a poor, miserable sinner ready for his eternal rest might gain entrance.

The heavy wooden doors reinforced with iron swung open, and Franz Josef's casket was taken inside and placed next to those of his ancestors.

After Uncle Shumi finished telling the story, he told me he had first heard it from his father, Karl Schwarcz, a devout Jew who saw beauty in the pageantry of another faith and another land, and who loved his Roman Catholic king with his Jewish heart.

In April 1989, in Washington's St. Matthew's Cathedral, I attended the requiem mass for Zita, the last Empress of Austria and Queen of Hungary, wife of Franz Josef's ill-fated successor Karl. She died in Switzerland at the age of ninety-six, and while she disliked Hungarians, whom she blamed for the collapse of her empire, she was my grandfather's last queen. I felt duty-bound to pay my respects.

The ceremony was austere and impersonal, yet moving. For the first time in my life, I had a chance to sing *Das Kaiserlied*, which was the Habsburg anthem and the concluding hymn of the mass. I could not help noticing that the anthem, a glorious, triumphant march by Haydn, contained not a word about any part of the empire besides Austria. To the Habsburgs and to Austrians, Hungary was, after all, a conquered land, a colony.

Yet I understand my grandfather, I say to myself, I understand. Franz Josef let us cultivate our gardens and made it easier for us to engage in trade and sell our produce. He was the first Habsburg monarch to attend the opening of our synagogues. His flawless performance at ceremonial functions—and he seemed to be genuinely pleased when greeted by Jews and blessed by rabbis—helped make our world whole.

In our hearts we knew that this stern, narrow-minded man who could never warm up to his one son, Rudolf (thoughtful, sensitive, though, of course, dissolute) and who disliked his nephew, Franz Ferdinand (rigid, cold, and aggressive), somehow, for some reason, had a tender heart for us Jews. Perhaps it had to do with the staunchness of our loyalties—to our faith, to the Torah, to our fellow Jews, and, certainly, to him. Or perhaps the reason was the primal, unquestioning cast of our allegiances, our loyalty to the notion of loyalty.

The Old Emperor made good the ancient promises of kingship: tranquillity and grace. Except for the first fifteen years, his reign was a golden afternoon of liberalism. By 1867, he had acceded to the demands of the revolutions of 1848—free press, free elections, and a generous measure of autonomy for those who did not wish to be Austrians. The same year saw the emancipation of Hungary's Jews.

But when I recall Franz Josef's words, "Keeping calm is the citizen's first duty," I feel rebellion welling up in my chest. Keeping calm—what a self-serving, anemic non-answer! What a reptilian stasis when compared to the grace of motion and emotion! No wonder that the youth of 1848 took to the barricades! It becomes clear to me that the civilization that Austria has represented for centuries to the lands to the east neither overcame nor understood the passions it tried to control. It relied shamelessly on its military might and its secret police, and sweet serenity became evident only during its decline and particularly after those fatal shots were fired in Sarajevo.

On the other hand, perhaps rebellion is a folly of youth, and its brief magical days offer a nation merely the illusion of being young. The high, impossible standards of youth are tempered in middle age, though they are never entirely forgotten. Like first love and other fierce loyalties of adolescence, a revolution leaves its mark on those who live through its heady days of freedom and its heart-rending finale. March 1848—like October 1956—is a sacred moment in time when people rising against tyranny were beautiful and powerful and pure. It is a youth that can never come again. At least not for the same generation.

What kind of a man was Karl Schwarcz?

He loved trees and wheat fields, horses and rivers. He cherished those parts of the Jewish liturgy that gave thanks to God for the abundance of life. He was proud of the rosebushes he selected for his front yard. They came in all hues, from lush scarlet through fey yellow to chaste white, and what mattered to him were strength of scent and profusion of blooms. He would not allow roses to be cut for vases indoors, but he had the spent petals collected in wicker baskets and brought inside the house, to be kept for fragrance and beauty, until they all dried up and turned brown. In his village and

116

In the early years of the century, vacationing Róza and Karl Schwarcz posed for this picture on the patio of their hotel in Abbazia, on the Adriatic coast of the Habsburg empire.

outside it, he walked the earth in praise of God and His creation. He thrived on travelling, and he tracked down new hybrid plants and agricultural technologies while making friends with all the different people engaged in such projects. But he loved equally the drama of homecoming. Each time he returned, he announced that regardless of the beauty and the wealth of the places he had visited, he was convinced that his village was God's own garden on earth. In his heart, the nomadic shepherd Jacob and the stay-at-home nest builder King Solomon were harmonious co-tenants.

On a fine sunny day each spring, Karl Schwarcz would decorate his best open carriage and his two best horses with long, brightly colored ribbons and then took his wife Róza— Rachel in Hebrew—and their children for a ride around all the lands he owned and leased to inspect the lovely fresh green stalks of the new wheat. "This is life," he would cry out, hug and kiss his wife, and then chant the prayer of thanksgiving with more than his usual considerable fervor. On a fine day during the summer, after the wheat fields had turned into a sea of golden waves, he would conduct another ceremonial tour.

But if something went wrong with the crops he would invent excuses and postpone the tour. He could never bring himself to tell bad news, particularly to his beloved wife. To perform that function, he had his brother Yankev, his favorite among his six brothers and one sister.

Karl Schwarcz did not have a good singing voice but he loved listening to music. When he hired people to work around his house, he conducted an unusual job interview. "Sing me your favorite song," he asked, and if the applicant sang well, he or she had a good chance of employment.

118

He had a coachman who was a drunk, an obsessive skirt-chaser, a lazy good-for-nothing whom everyone in the household would have liked to have seen dismissed. But my grandfather wouldn't listen to them because, he said, "When this coachman sings, the angels start to dance."

My grandfather lived at peace with his fellow man and refused to recognize an enemy. In 1915, he stood at the gate of his house in Gyulaj, waiting for the Russian prisoners of war that the government had decided to billet on his estate. The villagers stayed inside their houses and bolted their doors because·it was said that the Russians were fierce giants who had to be chained or they would go wild and attack people.

Karl Schwarcz welcomed the ragged, sorry group of twenty-five prisoners with a little speech in French, a language he had learned in school in Vienna. He chose French because he knew no Russian, but he had read, in Hungarian, Tolstoy's *War and Peace*, in which the officers spoke French. The Russians did not understand his words, but they understood their meaning.

He told the Hungarian guards to unshackle the prisoners and the guards obeyed. He shook hands with each prisoner as they dismounted from the horse-drawn wagon. He motioned them to follow him to the barn, a spacious and clean-swept place where the annual harvest celebrations were held. In the middle of the barn was a table, covered with a white cloth, offering plenty of food and drink. With both hands stretched out, he used his favorite phrase for an invitation, remembered well by his children: *Részesedjünk*—a simple, compact Hungarian phrase which means "Let us all partake."

The war was in its second year and the Habsburg monarchy's losses were high on the Russian front where most of the Hungarian soldiers fought, including many young men from Gyulaj. Most Hungarians blamed the Russians for instigating the Serbs, for plotting the assassination of Crown Prince Ferdinand, and for itching to fight a war. Nor did Hungarians forget that two generations earlier their revolution of 1848 was crushed by another czar, another Nicholas. Thus Russian prisoners of war in Hungary were accustomed to harsh treatment, and they were amazed by Karl Schwarcz's hospitality. They showed their appreciation by singing and dancing, which went on for several hours because they discovered that their host, who had never been to Russia, loved their music. The sounds of revelry lured some villagers out of their houses, and from behind the safety of the Schwarcz courtyard's picket fence, scores of them lined up to listen.

From then on, the two officers ate in the Schwarcz dining room every day, while the enlisted men, who had all been peasants before the war, were housed and employed on the estate and paid regular wages. One of the officers, a dapper lieutenant called Alexander and a journalist in civilian life, fell in love with Karl Schwarcz's eldest daughter Elza, then seventeen and the family beauty. As soon as her father learned of the lieutenant's interest, Elza was sent to an uncle for an extended visit. But the lieutenant stayed for many months as an honored guest, until his government exchanged him for a Hungarian officer.

Alexander's colleague had been a university student. Remembered as "the baby-faced Lieutenant Tyomkin," he courted Miss Laura, the young and innocent school teacher from a nearby town who earned extra money by taking care of the younger Schwarcz children during summer vacation. Tyomkin claimed to want to learn Hungarian, or perhaps that was only an excuse Miss Laura produced to explain why she spent so much time with him. After Tyomkin received permission to return home and left suddenly, Miss Laura committed suicide by jumping into the river Tisza.

Partly because of the example Karl Schwarcz showed, the villagers eventually accepted the Russians, some of whom acquired girl friends, married them, and chose not to return to Russia after the war. Their children and grandchildren are still in Gyulaj, and my mother, Anna, who has visited with them, reports that they know—it has been passed down to them—that the village once had a landowner who was the first to hold out his hand to the enemy.

Karl Schwarcz was a devout Jew who greeted with a prayer each sunrise and sunset. He respected the sanctity of the Sabbath and he celebrated all the holidays. But he did not press others to live up to his high standards. His lawyer, Aladár Elekes, a lifelong friend, was a Jew whom others considered godless because he kept only one holiday, Yom Kippur, the Day of Atonement. The lawyer is afraid to talk to his God on weekdays or even on the Sabbath; he can't face his Maker more than once a year, people said behind his back.

Every year, Karl Schwarcz invited Elekes to spend the day praying in the tiny synagogue of Gyulaj and to break the fast together. After the lawyer beat his breast, begged forgiveness for his sins, and completed the festive meal that began after the appearance of three stars in the sky, he went home to the county capital of Nyiregyháza and lived free of the many laws of Judaism for yet another year.

Some people thought it unseemly that a pious Jew like Karl Schwarcz should pray next to an apostate, shoulder to shoulder, prayer shawl to prayer shawl. Didn't Karl Schwarcz, the wealthiest landowner and thus the first citizen in the village and of its Jewish community, set a bad example to others who might then conclude that ignoring the laws of Judaism was permissible? From time to time, Karl Schwarcz was asked: "Will your friend Elekes ever repent and return to the faith?"

My grandfather's answer was the same, year after year: "Oh yes, it's possible. But if I ask him such a question, it will not make that happen one day earlier."

Every spring, shortly before Passover, Karl Schwarcz had his house whitewashed, inside and out. A design of 365 bouquets of flowers running in a strip around the dining room walls a few inches below the ceiling was also repainted in bright colors, except for one part right above the entrance door. This conspicuously unpainted section served as a reminder to him and his family that even though things were going well for them—and being able to paint the house every year was an indication of prosperity—such good fortune rested on uncertain foundations and might not last long.

Paint is the outermost layer of things, the surface. For matters of substance, Karl Schwarcz had other rules. He would only keep animals that were without a blemish, which is one of the original meanings of the word kosher. Of course, Jewish dietary laws were observed in his house, but he also gave away or threw out cups and plates that chipped or developed as much as a hairline crack. The Talmud did not require him to do so, and it did not occur to other Jews that there was anything wrong with flawed china or glassware. Insisting on such perfection was my grandfather's own personal rule, an extension of the rigor of the law of what is kosher.

On his trips to Vienna and Budapest, he liked to buy entire

uncut bolts of cloth and a gross of items such as glasses and plates. The needs of his large household and the average of two guests to a meal justified such purchases. But at the same time, he took extra pleasure in buying merchandise in an undivided entirety. His world was whole and he did what he could to keep it that way.

To harvest his wheat, every August he hired twenty-four men to cut the stalks with their scythes and twenty-four women to bind the stalks. He loved to watch the rhythmic cutting of a swath, done in unison and accompanied by an ancient chant, and the placing of the bundles of stalks at intervals as precise as pieces arrayed on a chessboard. After all the stalks were cut and bound, he had it announced in the village that the fields were open to those who wished to pick up whatever had fallen on the ground. Nor were the edges or corners of the fields harvested. In the Bible, the poor were entitled to such "gleanings," and Karl Schwarcz observed that rule.

In Gyulaj and elsewhere in the county, and even outside it, he bought land wherever he could and regardless of its geometrical shape or quality of the soil. But whenever possible, he negotiated and traded with his neighbors so he could end up owning a square plot, which was a strange caprice in a country of extended rectangular properties so often subdivided by heirs they are called "belts."

Perhaps his preference for a square had to do with the form of the first field purchased by his grandfather's grandfather in the early 1800s, which was duly recorded by the county even though Jews could not legally own land in Hungary until the 1840s. Uncle Shumi remembers that property as a perfect square of fourteen lovely, level acres plowed and raked smooth every fall, or twenty *hold* according to the Hungarian measurement, which represented considerable wealth and qualified one as a fairly well-to-do villager. A few hundred yards from the ancestral home in Derzs and surrounded by a ditch and a single row of locust trees, the plot was held in high regard by the family as its first acquisition of arable land, and it might have been the model for Karl Schwarcz.

But it is also possible that he was drawn to the equilibrium of a square, impressed by its emphatic and unmistakable power of symmetry. Even today, after land reforms and collectivization and now privatization again, his square plots, framed by locust trees, are left intact, and villagers born long after he died still know they were once his.

He had his estate organized in a production loop that was more than just self-sufficient. His potatoes, which grew into an abundance of large tubers in the porous, sandy soil, were turned into alcohol in the distillery he built in 1899, and whatever was left over after the distillery process was used to feed cattle, which grew and fattened quickly. The cattle also provided good manure, which was spread on all the fields every winter. Soil thus enriched yielded a larger crop of potatoes, as well as wheat and tobacco.

During the First World War, when other landowners demanded for their wheat and other produce higher prices from the military, Karl Schwarcz would not, saying he would not profit from the war. After the war began, he sold his potatoes to the military at the low, state-controlled price and would not take advantage of the higher prices for liquor and the increased demand for alcohol generated by the war.

Karl Schwarcz had a hunger for land that profit alone does not explain. He dreamed about owning land the way other people dream about acquiring emeralds or rare books. He even bought meadows and hillsides in hard-to-reach areas far from Gyulaj for which he had no immediate plans. Other entrepreneurs earned far greater profits by investing in industry and trade, but Karl Schwarcz would not be diverted from his focus. He paid no attention to warnings by his brother Yankev, who only leased land and who held to the centuries-old Jewish view that buying land was risky because it could easily be confiscated by jealous local lords or a hostile government.

My grandfather's halcyon time, known in Hungarian and German as "the blessed years of peace," began some twenty years after 1867, the year Franz Josef made peace with his Hungarian subjects and had himself crowned king of Hungary, and it ended decisively in 1914, when Franz Josef went to war against Serbia and Russia. Particularly between 1890 and 1910, Hungarian wheat and cattle fetched high prices on the European market.

"It was a time when whoever owned one acre of land longed to buy a second acre," wrote his eldest son, Shumi, in his memoirs. "Whoever owned ten acres wanted a hundred, and whoever inherited a thousand acres would have liked to acquire the entire country. This epidemic also infected my father."

Karl Schwarcz was born into an age of faith and hope. The vast majority of Jews still believed in the God of their fathers. In the Austro-Hungarian monarchy, an emancipated Jewish bourgeoisie believed in the irreversible march of progress as well. They worshipped the Zeitgeist of enlightenment and liberalism, and they admired the righteous Gentiles it produced.

In the 1880s, in the Hungarian village of Tiszaeszlár, not far from Gyulaj, Jews were accused of murdering a Christian girl to mix her blood in their Passover matzah, and in the 1890s in France, a republic proud of its motto of liberty, equality, and fraternity, a Jewish army captain named Dreyfus was sent to Devil's Island on trumped-up charges of espionage and high treason. But there were Gentile liberals like Károly Eötvös and Emile Zola who risked their careers—even their lives—to stand up for the Jews, and there were conservatives like Franz Josef who held up to his many nations the examples of Jewish industry and family cohesion. It seems bizarre now, but the Budapest-born Theodor Herzl, the founder of political Zionism, put his faith in right-wing Germans—Kaiser Wilhelm and the Kaiser's uncle, Friedrich, the Grand Duke of Baden—and when Herzl spoke of "the dream of a Jewish homeland in Palestine," he had in mind a German-speaking protectorate that would promote German civilization.

Anchored in his faith and in his land, Karl Schwarcz moved about with ease in a world of class, privilege, and etiquette. He did not seek the company of the wealthy and the powerful, but those who went to see him in Gyulaj were well received, and they included members of the Hungarian Parliament, aristocrats and, of course, officials and landowners of Szabolcs County. "He never put on any airs," said a nephew, Endre. He wore white shirts and black or dark gray suits that were old-fashioned but well-cut, and he did not shed the accent or the singsong cadence of his country.

To the noblemen who had owned their estates for centuries, it was reassuring to see that he was a traditionalist who emulated at least some features of the old patriarchal order. At the same time, he was a threat because he was an ambitious innovator, eager to try out new plants and machinery. He also spent more time with and was closer to his peasants than what other landowners thought wise or necessary.

His was a time of ambition, make-believe, and romance, of sweet cheap patchouli and cool subtle lavender, of lace and brocade, of refined mauve and garish red. Jews fresh from the ghettoes of Central Europe, or escapees from the czar's prisonhouse of nations, quickly adopted the fashions of Budapest and Vienna, Paris and Berlin. They mixed with the sons and daughters of families that had ruled over Europe for centuries. Some Jews comported themselves as oriental princes in disguise, outdoing in chutzpah what a descendant of Charlemagne could offer in plain snobbery. There were unforgettable schoolboy pranks and night-long waltzes, sentimental quatrains inscribed in diaries held under lock and key, and spring violets plucked during rendezvous that were dried and pressed and kept for a lifetime.

Jews climbing the ladders of financial or intellectual success both conformed to the rules and threatened to undo them. The fashionable operettas playing in Budapest and Vienna, composed and written by Jews like Leo Fall and Imre Kálmán, were about doddering archduchesses and smart hussars, irresistible Gypsy beauties and wise peasants, the newly rich getting richer and the old rich squandering their wealth. The motley characters mixed and matched splendidly—which was the delicious surprise that the audience loved to watch—but their traditional roles were often reversed, and caste and ritual ridiculed. Everyone laughed and applauded, particularly the ruling class whose endearing ineptness was the basis for the jokes.

In Budapest the man who set the standard for wit was the monocled Ferenc Molnár, whose play about an unwashed, brutish merry-go-round operator was reincarnated as the American musical comedy *Carousel*. Molnár's style was a heady compound of mayhem and compassion, Hungarian hau-

127

teur and Jewish self-mockery, local color and cosmopolitan glitter. Molnár and his friend Jenö Heltai wrote the sharpest light verse, for cabaret and theater. Heltai's cousin, Theodor Herzl, might have had theater on his mind when he developed his first plan to solve the problem that troubled him as a successful journalist in Vienna: despite all their demonstrable progress, Jews continued to stand apart in the Habsburg empire. The young Herzl wrote: "In the broad light of day, at noon on a Sunday, a solemn and festive procession accompanied by the pealing of bells shall proceed to the St. Stephen Cathedral in Vienna. There shall be no furtiveness and no shamefacedness, as hitherto, it shall be done proudly and with a gesture of dignity. . . . We, the intermediary generation, are to remain where we are; we shall stand by the faith of our fathers, but our children shall pass over to Christianity before their conversion can bear the character either of cowardice or of interested scheming."

Unlike some of his contemporaries, Herzl later rejected conversion, which earlier in the century the German-Jewish poet Heinrich Heine called "the passport to European civilization." To Karl Schwarcz and his family, conversion was an unthinkable betrayal of the self.

During the reign of Franz Josef, wealthy Jews willing to practice charity could easily become barons, the lowest title in the aristocracy, but a hereditary title nonetheless. Karl Schwarcz, who contributed to the building of the Catholic and Calvinist churches in his village and gave generously to other causes as well, was offered the honor. After the briefest of considerations, he declined. Attaching the title "baron" to his name would have violated his insistence on modesty.

The emancipation of Jews led to intermarriage. Heads shook and tongues wagged in 1899 when Móric Jókai, the immensely popular patriarch of Hungarian life and letters, married Bella Grósz, an aspiring, beautiful actress who happened to be related to the Schwarcz family. He was seventy-four and she was not yet twenty. It was more than a wedding of a Gentile and a Jew, or even of an old man to a young woman. It seemed like a jarring juxtaposition of the venerable noble Hungary and the garish new Hungary, and a challenge to the old order that shocked traditionalists, including my grandfather.

Jókai's more than one hundred volumes of novels and novellas painted a national gallery of heroes and villains, along with a supporting cast of thousands. Hungarians recognized themselves in his books and they sought to shape their lives so they would reenact his improbably romantic plots, which recalled the sagas of Dumas and Dickens.

Theater, too, was more than entertainment. It was a relatively new art form which held the nation in its thrall, particularly the younger generation. Even more than a Jókai novel, theater blurred the distinction between the real and the illusory, and a beautiful actress could become the country's alternative queen, with a court of admirers and a roster of lovers. The dark-eyed, dark-haired femme fatale Bella Grósz was a disturbing temptation that one poet compared to an unknown flower grown from a stray seed carried by the wind from a faraway land.

Karl Schwarcz, who devoured all of Jókai's works and who was fond of Bella Grósz as a relative, wished that the novelist and the actress had never met. He objected to intermarriage on the usual grounds: it means the loss of a Jew to his or her people. He also sensed that the Jókai-Grósz union helped to unhinge the orderly world he was born into and understood. He did not care for the theater; he saw that it captivated people, by offering an alternative reality and a possibility to evade one's true self.

He was too soft a man to forbid his two oldest sons to frequent the theater or to stop them from following fashion by sending bouquets to actresses and falling in love with them. Theater was the favorite genre of the carefree, playful new generation that embraced the pleasures of the moment and rejected their parents' preoccupation with eternity. Like film and television decades later, the stage rendered dreams of love and power visible and accessible, thus, in the view of the traditionalists, trivializing them.

Karl Schwarcz too was a dreamer, and he was born in a century and a county known for nourishing dreamers who dreamed while awake.

One odd piece of history stirred the imagination of his contemporaries, Jewish and non-Jewish alike. It was a recorded fact that many Jews had joined the ninth-century pagan Hungarian tribal confederation that rode across the Carpathian mountains from the steppes of what is now Russia, and conquered what is now Hungary and Transylvania. The Jews were Khazars, the remnants of a nation that once flourished in what is now southern Russia and the Ukraine, and whose rulers converted them to Judaism in the eighth and ninth centuries. According to Hungarian chronicles and local memory, many of the Khazars settled in the villages of Szabolcs County.

In the 1890s, friends and well-wishers suggested that the Schwarcz family point to its cemetery in Derzs and claim Khazar origins. Though the earliest legible headstones dated to the 1600s, there were many older headstones whose inscriptions had been erased by rain and wind and sand. Still more tombs had sunk deep into the soft sand. A little ex-

In 1915, the second year of the First World War, Uncle
Shumi, sixteen, with two Russian prisoners of war who were
billeted in his father's house in the village of Gyulaj. In the
window is Captain Alexander, who fell in love with Shumi's
eldest sister Elza, then seventeen. To Shumi's right is Lieutenant Tyomkin, who courted Miss Laura, a local teacher.

cavation might well prove that the cemetery was begun during the reign of the Royal House of Árpád, descendants of the chieftain Árpád who conquered Hungary in 896.

Around the time the nation celebrated its millennium in a frenzy of patriotic pride and ancestor worship, some family friends, Jews and Gentiles, were enthusiastic. Here was a good chance to prove that at least some Hungarian Jews, particularly those from Szabolcs County, had roots in Hungary as deep in time as their Gentile fellow citizens. Wasn't it heartwarming and soul-lifting, they argued, to consider that Jewish warriors helped to conquer the Carpathian Basin, settled in Szabolcs County, and thus played a respectable part in the nation's glorious genesis? Shouldn't there be more research into the subject, they added, and shouldn't a fine, thoughtful scholar expand the Khazar thesis, secure the imprimatur of the Academy of Sciences and the Ministry of Education, and have it cut into marble slabs and printed in school books as the nation's official history?

My grandfather and his brothers were embarrassed by the suggestions and could not bring themselves to endorse a revision of the past for the purpose of parading the enduring patriotism of Hungarian Jews. Karl Schwarcz was a flammable soul, and he liked spending time with dreamers, including those enamored of the Khazar thesis. But he looked ahead, not backward, and his dreams were grounded in the tangible.

In the first years of the twentieth century, my grandfather and his brother Yankev purchased a stone house in Jerusalem and rented it out to a rabbinical seminary for the token sum of one golden krone a year. They also sent and maintained there a pious cousin who supplied them with palm branches and citrus fruit for holidays and prayed for the souls of family members on the anniversaries of their deaths. But no one else in the family considered moving to Palestine. The Austro-Hungarian monarchy was their land of milk and honey, presided over by Franz Josef. Anti-Semites who disliked him called him the Judenkaiser—the Jewish emperor—and Jews believed that the Prophet Elijah had rewarded him with a long life.

After the Habsburg monarchy ended up on the losing side of the First World War, there were robberies and murders by roving bands of returning soldiers accustomed to using guns against the enemy and now ready to aim them at their countrymen. They were joined by peasants desperate for land and property they had been denied for generations.

There were two revolutions in Hungary that followed the First World War, and they mirrored Russia's February 1917 revolution against the feudal order and the October 1917 coup d'état by the Bolsheviks. The countryside swarmed with men who looted, pillaged, and burned and declared landowners' possessions as theirs from then on. As the richest people in the village, the Schwarcz family was advised to take refuge in the nearest small town, Nyirbátor, some ten miles from Gyulaj. It was not easy to persuade Karl Schwarcz that he and his family were in real danger, but in the end a high county official who was an old friend personally appealed to him, and he left.

When Karl Schwarcz learned that like so many other residences of the wealthy, his house, too, had been ransacked, he said, softly, "At least nothing was set on fire." (Many other houses and estates became victims of arson.) "Our front yard, always clean-swept, was strewn with straw, papers, trash, and broken pieces of furniture," his eldest son, Shumi, recalled in his memoirs. "The front door, wrenched from its hinges, was flat on the ground; next to it, like a symbol, lay our faithful dog Sheyem, shot dead."

When order was restored, the troublemakers were rounded up and sentenced to long prison terms. As part of their rehabilitation, they were taken to face the people they had wronged. Karl Schwarcz's youngest son, Bédi, remembers how a gendarme came to the house where the family stayed in Nyirbátor and asked that "the honorable Karl Schwarcz" please come out and talk to "the bandits who wrecked his property." My grandfather went outside and saw some fifty men, with hands ties behind their backs, kneeling in the dirt of the courtyard, and surrounded by armed guards.

"Sir, they are here to beg your forgiveness," the officer announced in a loud voice.

There was a rumble from the men. "Forgive us, sir, for what we have done. We are deeply sorry for the suffering and the damage we caused."

The officer then asked Karl Schwarcz if he might like to address the men.

"I cannot talk to people who are bound," said Karl Schwarcz, who recognized some of the faces. He asked the officer if the guards could untie the convicts. The officer did as asked.

"I still can't talk to them," Karl Schwarcz said. "I cannot talk to people who are on their knees." The officer commanded the group to get up.

Bédi, six at the time, stood next to his father, who was already very ill and frail and had only a few months to live. Bédi does not recall the words his father used in the brief speech that followed, but he remembers the gist, which was, "What happened, happened. Now let us start anew."

Upon returning home, Karl Schwarcz had all the broken pieces of furniture collected and had a cabinetmaker splice and patch them together. It was an expensive project, more expensive than buying new furniture, and this at a time when his financial resources were depleted. But Karl Schwarcz could not be talked out of it. He believed in repairing what could be repaired and in making whole again what was broken.

He refused to accept help from government officials—his old friends—who were anxious "to teach a stern lesson to the bandits" as well as to "those who had taken advantage of the chaos." He told the authorities that he wanted no house searched in the village and no villager punished. Instead, he had it announced in the village that those who "took for safekeeping" something from his house should bring it back by next morning and that there would be no questions asked. As for the dogs who were normally allowed to roam in the courtyard all night, "they would be securely chained," the message said.

In the darkness of the night, many, though by no means all, of the household goods were returned. During the nights that followed, additional items were left in front of the gate.

When Szabolcs County was occupied by Romanian forces in 1919, there was another wave of violence and theft. Among other items, Karl Schwarcz lost his favorite horse, a gray thoroughbred Appaloosa mare he had raised himself, which was requisitioned by a tall, elegant Romanian army captain who fell in love with her.

A few days after the captain rode off on her back, the horse galloped home, without a saddle, finding her way from the Romanian headquarters in Nyirbátor, some ten miles from

Gyulaj. Suspecting what had happened, the captain travelled to the village, found the horse, and took her away a second time. Two weeks later, the faithful animal appeared again at the Schwarcz gate. "She came home, running over God knows what roads, foaming at the mouth," my mother remembers. "She was covered with sweat. Nickering happily, she ran straight into her stall. Our indescribable joy ended only when the Romanians came and took her away again."

From the Romanians, the family learned that the horse had gotten loose more than a hundred miles from the village, in a Transylvanian town she had never been to—and yet she found her way home!

The captain was furious and said that this time he was taking the horse to the other side of the Carpathian mountains and he would make sure that she would never be able to run away again. Karl Schwarcz begged the captain to take another horse or some other valuable instead, but he got nowhere. The captain's pride had been hurt by the animal. He had to have her. The horse did not come home again.

According to Shumi's analysis, the collapse of Karl Schwarcz's estate had its origins in his indomitable optimism. As a child of nineteenth century romanticism, he trusted the forces of progress; as a Jew, he believed it was his duty to make the world a better place. When the harvest was good and the economy robust, which they were in the first forty years of his life, he used his profits to buy more equipment, such as the first steam-powered threshing machine in the county, and more land, and he took out large loans for what he could not pay in cash. He kept investing and mortgaging, believing that the harvests from improved seeds and superior fruit trees growing out of the soil that he kept enriching with animal manure, leaf-mold, and green manure would bring only higher yields and greater prosperity for everyone. What he did not take into account was war and the violence of war, which did not stop once the war was over.

While his soul suffered from the decline of his estate, which he had built up with such meticulous care, his body was brought down by a severe case of diabetes, which eventually not only immobilized him, but led to a festering of every cut and bruise. For instance, he never recovered from a leg wound that began as a scrape when he slipped while trying to help an injured soldier climb aboard a train. Doctors could not stop his decline. Insulin, which would have helped him, was not yet discovered.

One rabbi tried an ancient ruse. In an elaborate ceremony, he gave my grandfather, whose Hebrew name was Akiba, a new name, Chaim, meaning life, and everybody was supposed to call him by that name. The idea was that when the Angel of Death came looking for a man of a certain age and physical characteristics called Akiba, he would not find him. Chaim would fit the description, but there was no Akiba. Confused, the Angel of Death would leave without the soul he was supposed to take away.

As he lost weight and strength and could no longer walk about, he had his bed moved to the window where he could see the lilac hedge around his rose garden and catch a glimpse of the locust trees in the distance. These were trees he and his ancestors had planted, for soil conservation and for verdant beauty. My mother's last memory of her father has him framed by a window, looking for hours at the garden he designed.

In his last will and testament, dated April 20, 1919, his wish was that his seven children never sell the lands he had acquired or transfer to someone else the lands he had leased. "No matter how hard it is," he implored his children, "take care of the land yourselves. Do not scatter, my dear children—"

It was at this point that his handwriting, which became more agitated with every page of his will, came to a halt. There was still space at the bottom of page five, but he left it blank, and his last sentence is unfinished, with a forlorn dash as the last mark on the page.

Then, on page six, there is one more sentence, standing by itself: "My children owe an eternal debt of gratitude to Ignatz Klein—forever." Klein was the banker, and a lifelong friend, who arranged the loans for Karl Schwarcz's purchases of land.

Karl Schwarcz asked that his headstone be "two hands-breadths lower" than his father's and that in his case, contrary to the custom of cutting flowery praises into the marble, the white marble favored by the Schwarcz family should be left blank except for identifying him by his Hebrew name and his father's: "Akiba ben Shmuel."

On March 19, 1920, the day the Romanian troops withdrew from the county, a villager came running to tell him the good news in the hope that it would cheer him up. "Thank God," Karl Schwarcz said, managed a smile, then turned to the wall and died.

After the black flag appeared on the flagpole of the Schwarcz house, the priests of the Greek Catholic and Calvinist churches in the village paid prompt condolence calls on the widow and asked for her permission to toll the bells during the funeral. She agreed, but suggested that the priests also ask the rabbi, who was to officiate. The two priests travelled to Rabbi Moshe Taub, the great-grandson of Isaac

Taub, the renowned Rabbi of Kálló who had blessed Karl Schwarcz's grandfather's grandfather.

The rabbi, too, agreed to the unusual request, and all the church bells in Gyulaj and Derzs tolled as members of the family and friends, villagers and county officials took turns carrying the simple coffin of unplaned pine boards and assembled without nails, from Gyulaj to the family cemetery in Derzs, four miles away.

"Everybody wanted to carry the coffin at least for a short while," remembers his second daughter, Anna, my mother, then twelve. The mourners walked all the way to the cemetery on the ancient dirt road. Bringing up the procession were his horses, without riders or saddles.

After the burial, his widow and his children could not bring themselves to comply with his request for a headstone "two handsbreadths" lower than his father's. After discussions with the rabbi, the order went out for a headstone identical in size to his father's. Nor could the family accept the notion of a headstone that was silent on his character. They turned to the county's chief rabbi with the question: how could we have something inscribed on the headstone yet at the same time respect his wish not to praise him?

The rabbi, who had known him well, gave the matter some thought before he replied. He suggested the following words be incised and they were: "He was a dear and honorable man. Let his humble heart be his praise."

Among the mourners accompanying Karl Schwarcz's coffin were Gypsies from Gyulaj and Derzs. On occasion, they had worked for him, and the musicians among them played at the harvest celebration and on other festive occasions.

Karl Schwarcz was fond of Gypsies and recognized them

as another band of immigrants to the Carpathian Basin, another wandering tribe from the East in search of a Promised Land. He was intrigued by their view of the highway as their home and by the refusal of most of them to settle in one place and to build anything more enduring than an adobe shack. He recalled how Pest and other important towns of the realm had once taken pride in wresting such privileges from the king as the right to an independent decision, by the town elders, whether "to tolerate or not to tolerate Jews and Gypsies" within city limits. Such medieval right to admit or expel members of these two tribes survived until the middle of the nineteenth century.

Like other Hungarians—and quite a number of Jews among them—he had a weakness for the Gypsy violinist's melancholy songs about the intoxicating scent of lilacs in a May of long ago and the withering leaves of today, about loves never to be forgotten and the immortality of the soul. In the lyrics, the preferred season is autumn, or the last days of a languid summer, with the grape harvest about to begin. The words and the music are drenched with a perpetual longing, a wish to be elsewhere or to be someone else, yet everyone stays put, and nothing and no one changes.

Gypsy songs log an endless passage to the past, and it is a hundred, a thousand times more splendid than the present could ever be, and the future seems unnecessary, pointless, futile. Gypsy music is a liturgy for dreamers, and images such as a servant maid sweeping the street, or a red silk ribbon fluttering in the wind, acquire a meaning far beyond their mundane insignificance. That meaning is secret, carrying hints of wealth and happiness and eternity.

Karl Schwarcz appreciated the Gypsies' dialect of metaphors because he was attached to its earthy models: trees that grow old and suffer through storms like human beings; fading roses that illustrate the fate of beauty and glory; and swift horses that stand for impulses and galloping thoughts.

A skillful Gypsy musician makes people remember the best days of their lives. He must have a key to every heart and he must understand every genre of sorrow and joy, and when he plays someone's favorite song, with his violin close to the patron's ears, he plays for that person alone, and nobody else exists. For some, a favorite song may be joyous; for others, sad. Gypsies believe that behind crying is a far, far deeper emotion than behind laughter and that the finest souls are those who are fulfilled when they cry. It is also part of the Gypsies' accumulated wisdom that those who have tears in their eyes when listening to music give the largest tips.

As a young man, Karl Schwarcz made friends with a Gypsy musician, Elemér Sáray, then a fiery, nimble, and dapper youth—and a promising second violinist in one of the kingdom's finest bands that turned down repeated invitations to move to Budapest and Vienna. The band stayed in dusty, slow-moving Nyiregyháza, the capital of Szabolcs County and the first station on my grandfather's many travels. But Sáray also visited Karl Schwarcz in his village. According to the custom of the time, he put Sáray on a generous retainer, paying him a few gold pieces each year and sending him sacks of the finest wheat flour, jars full of goose fat, and a large goose for Christmas. He even became the godfather of Sáray's eldest son. After Sáray took over as the leader of the band, he accepted an invitation to Budapest, and by the time the First World War began, he was playing in the capital's best hotels and had acquired fame throughout the empire.

He was in his seventies, with a bent back and white hair, when Shumi spotted him sipping coffee in the Arany Bika—

The Golden Bull in Hungarian—then, as now, the leading hotel and restaurant in Debrecen, where the Schwarcz family moved after it lost all its lands. Sáray said that he could not forgive himself for not being present at Karl Schwarcz's funeral. But he had not been informed, he said, and even if someone had sent him a telegram, it would have taken him three days to reach Gyulaj from Budapest, too late for the funeral. Sáray asked if he could pay his respects to the widow. Shumi said he was certain that she would be delighted. Sáray picked up his violin sitting next to him on a chair, and, leaning on Shumi, he walked over to the house, some three blocks away.

Grandmother Róza embraced the old Gypsy and offered him the choice seat in the house, an armchair that had been her husband's favorite. Sáray said he was honored, and he did not seem to notice the smallness of the room and the reduced circumstances of the once wealthy family. "He had such soothing, silky manners," Uncle Shumi told me. "He was an illusionist, a prestidigitator, a magician. When he spoke with us, he somehow made it appear as if we were still living on our estate, as if our world was still whole."

Then Sáray noticed Karl Schwarcz's framed photograph on the wall. He got up, took his violin out of its case, positioned himself in front of the picture, and started playing Karl Schwarcz's favorite song: "Gone are the golden leaves of the quaking aspen." The song is about two messages. The first is inscribed on a withered leaf of autumn, and it says farewell to a lover. The other message, a response to the first, is written on a new leaf the tree has sprouted in the spring, which says: "God be with you, my love, I am being carried to my grave."

"My unforgettable mother wept, leaning on the commode,"

Uncle Shumi recalled in his memoirs. "My luckless sister Elza sobbed by the window, and I stood behind Sáray, deeply moved. I watched this sophisticated Gypsy playing a tune as if in a trance, first very softly with his bow, then picking the strings with his fingers, very slowly and thoughtfully. He ended the song suddenly, in a characteristically Gypsy fortissimo, and rested his bow on the ground.

"He took out his white handkerchief and wiped his tears. In a shaky voice, he apologized for the sadness he had caused. There is no excuse for insensitivity, he said, but this song was his farewell to the friend of his youth.

"With a gentle wave of his hand he refused my offer to accompany him back to the hotel. He put his violin back into its case and left the house without a word, his head cast downward."

Over the years, whenever I am in trouble, or feeling very good, I have gotten into the habit of taking out of a drawer my grandfather's gold pocket watch. My eyes feast on the calligraphy of his embossed monogram, an artfully intertwined *K* and *S*, surrounded by the design of an endless knot that fades out on the rounded rim. I feel the weight of the watch, its solidity. I wind it and listen to it tick. The sound is clear and self-confident. I push the button that swings open the cover, revealing an enamelled white face with slender, elegant Roman numerals in black. I think of the time it was made: 1889. My grandfather was twenty-eight and not yet married, Franz Josef was fifty-seven, and Franz Ferdinand stood next in line to the throne.

The watch keeps perfect time.

Grandmother Róza as a young woman.

8.
The Silences of Grandmother Róza

They shall have stars at elbow and foot;
Though they go mad they shall be sane,
Though they sink through the sea they shall rise again;
Though lovers be lost love shall not;
And death shall have no dominion.
DYLAN THOMAS, "And Death Shall Have No Dominion"

In my grandparents' house in Gyulaj, Grandmother Róza sat at the head of the table, and stood in the foreground of every family photograph. Thus did Grandfather Karl defer to his wife, disregarding the formal arrangement of their otherwise patriarchal world. For her husband, for her children, and even for her grandchildren, she was the soul of the family.

Uncle Anti says his mother came "from another time and from another world. Neither exists anymore, and her kind of person is extinct. She never raised her voice. She never used a harsh word—not with us, her children, nor with anyone else. She didn't scold us when we did something she didn't approve of. No dire warnings before our transgressions and no recriminations after. Even though we did give her plenty of grief. Plenty. She lived for her family, for us, not for herself."

Her Hebrew name was Rachel, and it is tempting to compare her to that biblical matriarch, a shepherdess who endeared herself to her future husband by taking tender care of her sheep. "A woman of consummate kindness," is how one grand-niece, Ági Békés, remembers her.

145

"She is our family's *shekina*," says my cousin Levente Thury, using the Hebrew word for the luminous presence that sanctifies an individual or a group or a place. (In theology, *shekina* means the immanence of God.) Levente was three years old when he last saw our grandmother, and his father, also named Levente, was the first Christian who married into the Schwarcz family. "She made the molds which shaped our parents, our uncles and aunts, and, eventually, us," argues Cousin Levente, a sculptor in Budapest. "She also created the grammar which gave structure to our best ideas. Together, the molds and the grammar made us a family, a certain kind of family. What she provided was invisible and inaudible, yet without those gifts, there would have been no form and no text."

A woman who spoke seldom but always in carefully chosen words, Róza Kaufmann was graceful, fragile, and other-worldly. Midwives and other wise old women who know the secrets of men and women praised the match with her earthy, talkative, and exuberant husband, Karl Schwarcz.

She liked to sit in the courtyard in the evening and trace the constellations in the sky. He loved an early morning stroll to observe the progress of his crops. While he seemed to be rooted in the soil, she appeared to be a guest, a visitor just passing through, even in her own house.

Her face had an oval shape; his was round. Her nose was thin and aquiline; his was chunky and straight. She had an abundance of thick hair, and a version of a widow's peak. His hair followed a rounded-off line on his forehead until he went bald in his early thirties. She was slim and wiry; he, stocky. She had green eyes; he, dark brown. Their genes mixed, yet it has been customary to classify their descendants as either a Kaufmann or a Schwarcz. While their eldest daughter, Elza, was a Kaufmann, all the other children were Schwarcz, and Schwarcz remained dominant for the next two generations.

After her husband died and the family estate was auctioned off and she moved to a rented house in the town of Debrecen, her children and other members of the family often found her crying softly to herself while reading a book or working on a piece of lace or just sitting in a chair, alone in a room, thinking. Having gone to a high school run by nuns—not unusual for wealthy Jews who were traditionalists yet wanted a superior secular education for a daughter—she had learned to appreciate the poetry of Goethe, Schiller, and Heine. She was also a devout Jew who prayed every day, particularly for her children.

She was shielded from the problems of everyday life, first by her parents whose late child she was, and by three active and ambitious older brothers who doted on their only sister and cherished her tender femininity, then by her husband who was in love with her through the twenty-five years of their life together and could not bring himself to tell her any bad news, and finally by her children who went to great lengths to present her only the bright side of things. Nominally, she was in charge of the household, but in fact things were done for her, and with a minimum of consultation because everyone knew what she wanted and how she wanted it.

When she married Karl Schwarcz, a landowner in Gyulaj, in 1895, she was twenty-three and without any experience in running a household. She too was born in a village, Töke-terebes, but when she was little her parents moved to the small town of Ungvár, now part of Russia and called Uzh-gorod, where she grew up. In Gyulaj, she suddenly found

herself in charge of a large village household with dozens of
servants who cleaned and cooked and washed, prepared fires
in the kitchen and in the tile stoves in the dining room and
the bedrooms, and took care of the horses, the cattle, and
the barnyard.

Because Gyulaj was close to Derzs, where her husband's
family's ancestral home had been turned into a synagogue,
and because of her husband's hospitality and popularity, the
Schwarcz family usually gathered in Gyulaj. The rituals mark-
ing the anniversaries of the deaths of the Schwarcz parents
were also held in the house in Gyulaj, with more than a
hundred guests: the families of the seven sons and the one
sister who said Kaddish, the prayer for the dead; other relatives who came to pay their respects; rabbis who discussed
Talmud in honor of the departed soul. Finally, there were
dozens of poor Jews from throughout the county who were fed
the same sumptuous meals but could not be squeezed into
the dining room. They ate at a long table in the courtyard
and listened through open windows to the rabbis seated in
the dining room. The poor, as well as the rabbis, left the
following evening with envelopes filled with bank notes that
the Schwarcz brothers distributed in memory of their father
or mother.

Everywhere Grandmother Róza went in Gyulaj, she saw flocks
of large, plump, snow-white geese. When left alone, they
were as dignified as old peasant women, but when disturbed,
they were indignant, squawking like mere chickens and hiss-
ing like snakes. They wandered through the streets, foraged
in ditches rife with worms and weeds, and floated on waters
left behind by the last flood of the river Tisza. Unlike their

wild cousins, domesticated geese could only fly for a few yards before being brought down by their weight.

The goose had become the prime fowl in Hungary nearly four centuries earlier. It was made popular by those who provisioned the armies of the Turkish sultan and who had to rely on some animal other than the pig, as forbidden to Moslems as to Jews. The suppliers also commissioned peasants to plant the goose's favorite grain, maize, that wondrously productive New World import. Perhaps because some of the sultan's suppliers were Jewish or perhaps because of the fondness Hungarian Jews developed for goose meat, the goose became identified in Hungary as the Jewish bird, and to this day the word for the person raising or selling geese, *libás*, is an epithet for Jew.

The Schwarcz estate kept as many as two thousand geese, which provided the principal staple of meat, considered by many in Hungary the tastiest of all meats: rich in texture, supernally crisp when roasted, and adapting well to a wide array of spices. Geese also supplied the cooking fat, off-white in color and with the consistency of snow, which stood in the pantry in metal containers the size of small barrels and enamelled in bright blue. With an average goose yielding as much fat as twenty, even thirty hens, the goose proved to be a wise choice as the main fowl, and its fat was recognized as incomparably superior in taste to that of the chicken.

Another celebrated goose product was its down, as soft as puffs of smoke and almost as weightless, yet warmer than sheep's wool or fox fur. After they were washed and dried in the sun, the great clouds of white goose down were stuffed into comforters and pillows, and no young village girl would think of getting married without having enough of them for her marriage bed and for the guest room. To this day, my mother, Anna, has comforters filled with goose down from Gyulaj, encased in satin covers that have been replaced a few times.

But the jewel of the goose trade and the pride of the Schwarcz estate was the goose liver, *le foie gras* admired by the French, a nation of liver fanciers, as the world's tastiest and regarded in Hungary as a great delicacy, particularly among Jews.

Winter was the prime season for eating goose, which warms one's insides a way no other meat does. As soon as ice appeared on the roads, the Schwarcz household sent out horse-drawn wagons to distribute gifts of goose liver to relatives and friends, favorite rabbis, and county officials and business contacts. Each package was in a glass container carefully wrapped in white linen and shielded in a wicker basket. Each goose liver, the brown of Hungarian bread crust outside and the color of rye bread inside, was encased in the fat in which it had been fried. The flavor had to be delicate and the consistency a little harder than butter. As for size, the larger the liver the more it was appreciated—and the greater the glory for the household that produced it.

The tried and tested way to get a large and flavorful liver was by overfeeding a goose with corn until its liver became enlarged, a protective reaction that soon turns into illness. The overfeeding was done by village women who sat on wooden benches in front of their houses, in groups of two or three or more. They chatted as each woman held down with one arm a goose, which tried its best to get away, while the other arm was busy forcing corn down the bird's long neck.

Grandmother Róza was outraged. The goose is a beautiful bird and deserves better treatment, she thought. It seemed

Róza and Karl Schwarcz on vacation,
in the early years of the century.

to her that a flock of wild geese soaring in the sky in their perfect formation of the letter V was nothing short of an ode to the idea of passage from one world to another. She told her husband that force-feeding geese was cruel and that the sight of village women ramming fistfuls of corn down the throats of the birds was unedifying and ignoble. In short, she couldn't tolerate anyone in her household brutalizing geese.

My grandfather liked geese too—he was fond of all animals—but he had seen geese force-fed all his life and it never occurred to him that the practice might be considered cruel. He was also concerned about what recipients of his goose liver might say when they tasted a small and possibly less flavorful liver. After all, there was a reputation to maintain, and it would be an embarrassment to the house of Róza and Karl Schwarcz to start producing inferior goose liver.

On the verge of tears, Grandmother Róza expressed her conviction, born in the moment she said it, that without force-feeding the liver would be just as large and just as tasty.

Her husband doubted that, as did all the village women who were paid to work with the geese who were also unhappy with the thought of losing an excuse for all those pleasant hours of conversation. But the landowner accepted his bride's argument, and her word became the law. In the summer and fall of 1895, not a single goose was force-fed on the Schwarcz estate. Winter came, and when the geese were butchered, people could not believe their eyes and their palates: the livers were a little smaller but just as flavorful as before, which was considered something of a miracle.

The word spread through the village faster than a goose hops. Some villagers went as far as to claim that the livers of geese not force-fed were superior. The new mistress insisted that no miracle was involved. Nothing of the sort. The good results came from treating geese humanely, which was the only way to treat animals.

When Grandfather Karl died, in 1920, Grandmother Róza was only forty-eight, and her face still had that ethereal glow that had made her appear in her youth as dreamily romantic as one of those women who inspired Goethe. As a widow, living in Debrecen, the only colors she wore were black and dark gray. Once a week, she called on relatives in the middle of the afternoon, and she was home before dark, except when she went to synagogue, accompanied by her eldest daughter, Elza, or on the rare occasions when her brother or a niece talked her into seeing a classical drama in the theater. Though the family's trusted matchmaker suggested that she marry again—and her brother and favorite cousins, and even her own children agreed—she would not even consider the thought, let alone permit a candidate to enter her house. God had given her the perfect husband, she said, and nobody could ever come close to him. Now she had their children, the youngest of whom was only seven and the oldest twenty-two at the time of their father's death, to raise and give away in marriage.

Of the thirteen she had borne, seven children, three daughters and four sons, survived to adulthood. Each of her deliveries was difficult, and her labor often lasted several days, despite the prayers and amulets offered by the Rabbi of Belz. For the last few childbirths, a specialist was brought from Budapest to assist the family doctor and the village midwife.

Traditionally, Jewish women in labor are allowed, sometimes even encouraged, to shout and curse. Some pious Jews hire young rabbinical students to pray aloud outside the door of the delivery room to strengthen the mother's spirit, as well

Uncle Levente, in the 1950s, the first Christian to marry into
the Schwarcz family.

as to make sure that her curses and pledges never to have another child do not reach God's ear but are drowned out by the sounds of prayer. In Grandmother Róza's case, there was no such need. She bore her pains quietly, and she always said she looked forward to having her next child. Her husband either paced in front of the door or circled around the house, chanting the psalms of David.

Though women of her social status often relied on wet nurses, she insisted on nursing her children. When her youngest, a son by the name of Bédi, ran away to what was then Palestine at age eighteen, she blamed herself. She maintained that Bédi's decision to leave his family and country had its origins in her not being able to nurse him, as she had nursed all the others.

In his last will and testament, Karl Schwarcz asked his children to remember their mother's welfare as their "first and foremost concern." He added: "Otherwise I would not be able to rest in the grave." He even had his eldest son, Shumi, swear it, "even though he knew it was not necessary," as Shumi noted in his memoirs. The children complied with their father's wish. They all lived with her until they married and then they visited her nearly every day or wrote to her every week if they moved to Budapest.

But life in the town of Debrecen was not as simple as life in the village of Gyulaj, where the Schwarcz family had been a class apart, where the outside world came to its doorstep, and where some guests could be considered candidates for marriage while others clearly were not. In Debrecen, the Schwarcz boys and girls were newcomers without much social standing. They worked in offices or learned trades, and restrictions concerning friends could not be maintained.

Mara, the youngest daughter, fell in love with Levente, a Gentile, the son of the Calvinist priest in the village of Kisar, a few miles from Gyulaj. Levente too had studied for the priesthood, but was lured away by journalism. They met in the newspaper office where she was in charge of advertisements and he was the editor-in-chief. On several occasions, Shumi used stern language in trying to talk his sister out of going out with Levente, and her other older brother, Mishi, solemnly threatened to defend her honor by challenging Levente to a duel. Mara would not listen to Shumi, and Levente smiled and explained to Mishi that he opposed martial arts and disliked militarism of any kind.

Grandmother Róza didn't try to dissuade Mara from marrying outside her faith, but her silence hung as heavy as the darkest storm cloud. Mara knew how her mother felt—how could she not?—but she was in love with a gentle soul, a writer of thoughtful prose, a man as handsome as a movie star. Could anything else matter?

"It's not enough that he is a Christian, but he is not going to be able to earn a living," Grandmother Róza confided to a cousin. "Journalists earn little and always lose their jobs."

"Don't worry," said the cousin, trying to comfort her, "he can always go back to being a priest."

The marriage took place—it was a civil ceremony—and the new son-in-law assured his mother-in-law that her daughter would remain Jewish and that he was looking forward to having his wife light candles on Friday night. He explained he was in favor of celebrating every holy day of every religion and that he was uplifted by every sort of sacred book, but that he felt particularly close to Judaism and to the Old

Testament. He had studied Hebrew in the Calvinist seminary, and he was fascinated by the "magic simplicity" and the "lapidary beauty" of the holy language.

After Levente married Mara, he was invited to celebrate Passover in Grandmother Róza's house. As the eldest son, Shumi was in charge of the ceremony but he kept having problems with the Hebrew text—he was the first one to admit that his years of Hebrew training had been wasted on him. Levente asked if he could try reading a portion. He did so well that he was asked to take over the service—the commemoration of Israel's exodus from Egypt—which he did with skill and feeling.

By the time little Levente was born, in 1941, Grandmother Róza quietly announced to relatives who were keeping their distance from the Christian in the family that she loved her son-in-law as her own son.

As the editor of a local daily called Független Ujság, Hungarian for Independent News, Levente was active in the non-communist, strongly anti-Nazi left. He was among the first in Debrecen to hear stories about Nazi extermination camps, but few people believed the rumor. Levente faced a family opinion that was firm and unanimous: such a thing was simply not possible.

Uncle Levente was among the first to be arrested when the German army marched into Hungary on March 19, 1944. He survived the Gestapo interrogation, took part in the resistance movement after he was released, and for the three years of Hungary's postwar democracy he was a journalist and a politician active in the left-of-center Smallholders' Party, the country's largest political organization until it was dissolved by the communists.

After the Second World War, the youngest brother, Bédi, then living on a kibbutz in Palestine, wrote to the family, urging them to join him. But Levente was the only one who endorsed the idea. He wrote a long letter to his brother-in-law, explaining his excitement over the possibility of living in the Land of the Bible, in a reborn Jewish State. But his wife, Mara, and her brother Mishi wouldn't hear of leaving Hungary, my parents were afraid of starting a new life, my mother's younger brother, Anti, was still a prisoner of war in Russia, and Shumi said he would go only if the majority decided in favor of an exodus. In the end, only about ten cousins left.

Under the Stalinist regime, Uncle Levente's articles could not be published. He was blacklisted and the secret police watched him and called him in for monthly interrogations. In order to keep himself and his friends out of trouble, and not to get his friends in trouble, he stopped meeting with people outside the family. During the revolution of 1956, he linked up with his old friends, but the days of freedom were too short to launch a newspaper. In 1958, when he was only sixty-three, he fell seriously ill. Spending time in the custody of the secret police forces of two dictatorships had impaired his health, but now it was his spirit that gave way. He seemed suddenly to lose interest in living. The doctors said that his heart and lungs, though weak, would still hold out if only he had the will to live.

When he felt the end near, he asked to say good-bye to every member of his family, which meant the Schwarcz family. His parents had died years ago; he was an only son and had no cousins in Budapest. One by one, everyone came to his hospital room, and he had a kind word for each relative. A few hours before he died, he asked his brothers-in-law Shumi and Mishi, his two best friends, to hold his hands and recite the Kaddish, the Hebrew prayer for the dead.

Grandmother Róza was always sending gifts. In the last twenty-four years of her life, she could only afford small presents, but she kept sending them. It was not a habit she would or could give up.

The last gift my mother received from her came from the Debrecen ghetto where the authorities had interned the Jews so their subsequent deportation could be carried out more efficiently. The person who delivered it said that Grandmother Róza intended it to cover her daughter's head and keep it warm. It was a kerchief, a twenty-inch-square piece of flimsy cotton cloth, in two tones of light brown, with a modest design of stylized flowers against a backdrop of waves. What has puzzled my mother for nearly fifty years is that the kerchief had a long rip, and one corner of it, the size of a hand, was torn off. She has never been able to decipher why her mother sent her such a badly damaged gift.

As I look at the kerchief, which my mother has treasured, I think of my grandfather Karl who, in a golden age that now seems farther away than the heavens, was able to lay out his lands in the shape of perfect squares and who could afford to insist that a cracked or chipped cup or plate be thrown away immediately.

When I last saw her, in 1943, Grandmother Róza was seventy-one and I was six, but it seemed to me she was much older, as old as the rabbis of long ago whom she talked about in the stories she told me when she put me to bed—and that she was just as defiant of the Angel of Death as they had been. If I had known the word, I would have called her immortal.

For years, I refused to believe that her life had ended in an Auschwitz gas chamber. "But how can you be sure she is dead?" I kept asking my mother. "There is not enough evidence. Maybe she is still alive somewhere. She must be alive." No one in the family argued with me; my outbursts provoked only sighs. For several birthdays after 1944, I received presents, each with a note signed by Grandmother Róza, and in my mother's familiar handwriting.

After Nazi Germany collapsed in 1945, the Allied forces repatriated survivors of the concentration camps. Hungarian Jews were first sent to Budapest where, in a cavernous old building near the center of town, they were given food and clothing, and they left word how relatives and friends might find them.

Two or three times a week, my mother and I took the tram to the Pest side of the city to visit the building, which was the color of dust. We elbowed our way through the milling people, many of them holding in their hands photographs and repeating the names of the people they were looking for. Everyone was searching faces and asking questions of strangers, such as "Which camp did you go to?" When on occasion relatives or friends stumbled upon one another, shouting and sobbing added to the din, and others tried to catch a glimpse of those reunited and some wondered aloud if they too might be that happy one day.

The first place in the building everyone went to was an enormous bulletin board on which large letters asked *"Ki tud róla?"*—a laconic phrase, meaning "Who knows something about him or her?" There, people tacked up inquiries about missing relatives, in the hope that someone might pencil in a few words such as "I saw him alive after liberation." My mother put up a short list beginning with her mother and adding about a dozen or so more names, each with nickname. age, physical description, and last address.

After my mother found people from her mother's transport who told us how she perished, we still checked once a week. My mother could not quite bring herself to believe the eyewitnesses who came to include her brother Anti's wife, Clara. Besides, there were other relatives to look for. For most of 1945, we visited the gray building at least once a month.

Then my mother gave up.

In 1988, as he lay dying in a Budapest hospital, Shumi's last wish was that his sister-in-law Clara tell one more time the story of his mother's journey to Auschwitz at the end of June 1944.

She sat in a corner, Aunt Clara said, with Shumi's five-year-old daughter, Kati, in her lap much of the time. In the three days of the train ride, she only talked to her granddaughter—and her words were "soothing." Other people prayed, cried, complained, shouted, went mad, or quarrelled over who would drink first from the bucket of water they received once a day, or over the use of the other bucket they were given. She was silent. Upon arrival in Auschwitz, she was promptly directed to the left, to the gas chamber. Determined not to leave her, her daughter, Elza, followed her, even though she was told to go to the right, to work. Granddaughter Kati was also sent to the left, but because her mother, Agnes, did not want to leave her, they went together to the gas chamber.

"Suddenly, I was all alone," said Aunt Clara, then in her early twenties, who was sent to work in a munitions factory.

Our family no longer commemorates the days on which our parents and grandparents died. That feast of memory was dropped from our calendar after Grandmother Róza left us.

Sometime in 1944, about the time Grandmother Róza was forced to move into a ghetto surrounded by barbed wire and police, my mother offered God a deal: she would keep the Jewish law only if her mother came out of the war alive. After Grandmother Róza did not return from Auschwitz, my mother stopped saying her prayers and declared the dietary laws null and void. My father, Aladár, never an observant Jew, went along, as did the rest of the family.

No one could take Grandmother Róza's place and no one has tried. We, her children and grandchildren, live in the shadow of her memory. We remember the way she sat in her favorite armchair—made of bent wood, with a seat of woven cane—in the courtyard of her house in Debrecen, examining the daisies, the rosebush, and the lilacs, while waiting for her children to come home. Or we remember the way she promptly put down a book or her lacework the moment a grandchild called out to her or asked to sit on her lap.

We tell stories about our dead. Who would we be without calling the roll of relatives burned, hanged, and shot?

But in Grandmother Róza's case, there is no story that someone could tell to sum her up, to help us remember her. Her children merely repeat: *Anyukám*—which means "my mother"—and my cousin Levente and I say *Omama*—Viennese for grandma—which is what she liked us to call her.

162

That's all we say, and we have said it countless times these past five decades in the form of a sigh, as a fraction of a prayer, as an incantation.

Anyukám.

Omama.

In 1918, Great-uncle Yankev with his grandson Sándor. In his will two years later, Yankev left Sándor one of his sets of the Talmud. Sándor was killed in Auschwitz in 1944.

9.

A Man of Perfect Piety

It is to be all made of fantasy,
All made of passion, and all made of wishes;
All adoration, duty, and obedience,
All humbleness, all patience, and impatience,
All purity, all trial, all observance.
SHAKESPEARE, *As You Like It*

I have looked for him all my life: the Good Brother. There when called, and never tired, never bored. Loving and smart. Strong and compassionate. A wise counselor to the soul and a pragmatic problem solver. A man of action who also knows how to listen and what to say when action is not the answer. And if all else fails, he sings in a lovely voice that lulls pain and soothes the conscience.

My grandfather Karl was fortunate in having such a brother in Yankev, five years his senior, and unmistakably his favorite among his six brothers, even as Karl was Yankev's favorite. My grandfather looked up to Yankev as a superior steward of the land and as a craftsman in allocating charity. Yankev supported my grandfather in his many ventures—though no one remembers if Yankev ever needed any help from him. There was no problem that each did not discuss with the other.

The two brothers set up their households in villages ten miles apart. They often travelled together, particularly to Germany, where they indulged their shared passion of discussing and buying superior new hybrid plants and the latest in farm machinery. They died in 1920, within three months of each other, both of them from complications arising out of diabetes.

Yankev fathered ten children, five boys and five girls. Of the scores of cousins in my mother's generation and mine, Yankev's descendants have always been the closest to us—and we told them. During holidays, Yankev and my grandfather took turns visiting each other, taking along the entire family, and out of their eventual total of seventeen children, some were invariably left behind or "traded" for weeks, sometimes months, and on a few occasions, for a whole school year. My mother remembers that the great treat of her childhood was being allowed to stay in Uncle Yankev's house, or having some of his children stay with her. One of her younger brothers, Anti, was the proverbial bad boy who at home was often punished with "a jail sentence" in a shack that stored farm equipment. He recalls how in his uncle's house in Vaja, Yankev had him do somersaults and cartwheels, then judged his performance and paid him a penny if he did well, at the end of which Anti was too exhausted and seduced by pennies to get into trouble.

In dealing with the outside world my grandfather was liberal and open-minded, trusting people and chance and, above all, Providence. Yankev, however, tended to be conservative and cautious, spending his time on the fine print and insisting on stringent conditions. In the Talmud, these two inclinations are represented by the House of Hillel and the House of Shammai, and out of the debate between the rabbis of these two schools of thought comes a thoughtfully balanced judgment, which is the raison d'etre of the Talmud.

Yankev had the best singing voice in the family. It was a powerful, vibrant, resonant bass that suggested the sounds of a cello, and following his bar mitzvah, Yankev always led his brothers in prayer, passionately and flawlessly. My uncle Shumi remembers him with his large prayer shawl, white with silver stripes, covering his head and his voice carrying across the room. "I can still hear Uncle Yankev's velvet voice," another one of his nephews, Endre, told me half a century after Yankev's death. "His voice came from his soul and it entered your soul. It is a voice that I will hear until the day I die."

Among his brothers, Yankev was the most fervent in his devotion to the letter and the spirit of the faith. He was also the best qualified agronomist, and the first in the family to learn the sophisticated strategies of tending grapevines.

One of his granddaughters I was close to in my childhood gave me a fading carbon copy of his last will and testament, which he signed on June 20, 1920, five days before his death, at the age of sixty-four. In it he noted in the first paragraph that the date was also the first anniversary of the death of his second son, Andor. What Yankev did not mention was that Andor had been a captain in a hussar regiment, killed in one of the last battles of the First World War. Becoming an officer in a hussar regiment, heir to a daredevil, swashbuckling Hungarian military tradition dating back to the Middle Ages, was not a typical career for a pious Jew raised on the debates of the Talmud. Nevertheless Yankev, bookish, stocky, and about five feet six inches tall, was proud of the dashing, athletic Andor who was nearly six feet tall, and while the father did not encourage the son's pursuit of a martial career, he did not oppose it.

"Andor volunteered and was given the rank of an officer because he looked like one," says one of his nieces, Agi, citing her mother who cried her heart out on the occasion. "He had no military training or even a high-school diploma, but he had the bearing and the manners of the gentry, and the gentry was supposed to know how to wage war." Andor did his soldiering with great gusto and demonstrated bravery on the battlefield, for which he acquired a number of decorations. Except for an affair with a beautiful Viennese actress whom he wanted to marry—which led to unauthorized absences from the army, a reprimand from his commanding officer, and, finally, his father's stern and effective command to cease and desist—Andor remained to the end an exemplary hussar and an observant Jew.

As is customary among Orthodox Jews, Yankev Schwarcz's last will and testament consisted of two parts, the "ethical" and the "financial."

The financial will distributed his considerable wealth in farm equipment, savings accounts, and personal effects, which, he repeated and emphasized, were to be shared equally by all his children. Such evenhandedness was unusual among traditional Jews at that time. Jewish custom favored giving the eldest son half of the inheritance, with the other half to be distributed among the rest of the children, with sons often receiving more than daughters.

Yankev seemed afraid that the principle of sharing equally might be contested, or perhaps he only wanted to make certain that there would be no arguments. He stipulated that in case any dispute developed over any part of his last will and testament, it must be argued before five arbitrators: two picked by each side and a fifth agreed upon by the four, and that, if possible, all the arbitrators should be drawn from the ranks of our large family. Under no circumstances might the arbitrators' decision be challenged. In one long and legalistic sentence, Yankev warned—and I can almost see him wagging his finger in the air—that if somebody challenged or did not accept the arbitrators' decision as binding, or otherwise showed any disinclination to carry out any aspect of the will, he or she should henceforth be cut off from the family and no longer be considered a brother or sister. Then Yankev unsheathed his ultimate weapon: "As for me, I protest in advance that any such troublemaking child of mine should ever visit my grave."

He distributed a few items according to their traditional, gender-defined functions. To three of his grandsons, sons of his eldest daughter, he bequeathed his seventeen-volume edition of the Talmud, a relic he had purchased from the estate of a renowned rabbi. He left a new deluxe edition of the Talmud to his fourth and youngest grandson, Shándor, fathered by one of his sons, "in the confident hope that he too will study it." As for his silver candlesticks, each pair had long been designated for respective daughters.

All his other possessions were to be distributed by lottery. They included two Torah scrolls (normally used in synagogues but occasionally purchased by wealthy Jews for the home); a silver pointer or "hand," with which he kept track of the line he was reading in the Torah; a seven-branched silver menorah; a silver cup for Shabbos which had been used by the Rabbi of Belz in Galitzia, whom he and his brother Karl often consulted; another silver Shabbos cup that had once belonged to a prominent local rabbi who had been his friend and advisor; a little silver "spice tower" that contained sweet spices to remind people of the glory of Shabbos after the sun went down on Saturday night; a gold watch that he might have received from his parents for his bar mitzvah; a scroll of Esther which was read aloud once a year when the holiday of Purim was celebrated; a Passover Seder plate for the Passover ceremony made of wood that had grown in Jerusalem; and a box for keeping a citron, also made of wood from Jerusalem.

Yankev's "ethical will," neatly subdivided into ten clauses and addressed to his children, offers glimpses of what sort of man he was and how he sought to involve his children in the exercise of charity.

He began by composing a stiffly correct telegram in German, to be sent by his children to Jerusalem upon his death, in order that a poor, pious relative he supported there could start praying for his soul immediately. Then Yankev's local rabbi was to write a registered letter with detailed instructions to the same poor relative in Jerusalem, to make sure that no mistake had been made in the telegram and that there would be no mistake in praying for his soul on the appropriate date in the Holy City for years to come.

In the next clause, Yankev offered in one brief paragraph an object lesson to his children in practicing comprehensive, long-range charity. He asked that during the first year after his death they hire, and "honor with decent pay," a few poor, pious Jews to study the Talmud all day and pray for his soul in the morning and evening. Each of these scholars was also to be given at least a cord of hardwood for the winter, and they were to be reimbursed for the cost of getting the wood to their homes and having it split.

Then came a list of forty-seven direct recipients of Yankev's philanthropy: first, poor Jews in twenty communities he had visited at one time or another, then nine rabbis and seven relatives; the rest were deserving individuals and religious foundations. The largest donations went to his older brother Zhigmond, who had gone bankrupt, and their one sister, Fanny, who had lost her husband and was without any income. The communities he favored most were those where his children were born or in which they had celebrated their weddings. He was most generous to rabbis he knew and respected, as well as to cousins listed as "blood relatives." But he seemed to have thought of everyone he had come into contact with. He left one hundred koronas, the smallest monetary unit of his charity, to the poor in each of the twelve mineral-spring spas where he had gone to refresh his "much-tired nervous body" and for treatment of his diabetes. The total he distributed to charity was the tidy sum of 100,000 koronas, roughly the equivalent of $10,000 today, which was a very large sum in those days and in that part of the world.

One imagines he must have spent many hours, if not days, in preparing the list of his beneficiaries. The amounts and his explanations make it clear that in each case, he carefully balanced the strength of his affections against the needs of the recipient. In an elaborate commentary suggesting the rhythm of a passage in the Talmud, he observed that giving charity to the poor had always been the greatest joy of his life. "Let us have trust that our God—who does not stay in debt to anyone for long—will pay you back richly for what I have given," he wrote. He took issue with unnamed wealthy Jews who left money to their family rather than to the poor and who then claimed that they loved their family more than they loved strangers. "I protest against such a skewed argument," Yankev wrote, and one could almost hear him raise his voice, "I refuse to believe there is anyone in the world who loves his children as much as I do." Yankev made it clear that it was precisely because he loved his children and was concerned about their welfare that he was letting them earn heavenly credit from his charity.

He reminded his family that even though he had lost his wife ten years earlier, when he was fifty-four, he had never remarried because he "did not have the heart to take home a strange woman who would reign over and annoy my dear children." Here he had to interrupt his writing, he noted, "because I broke out crying."

Then came another request for charity: that on the anniversary of his death and that of his wife, all his children who maintained their own households were to serve dinner to ten, or at the very least three, poor, pious Jews and provide gifts to each. He entrusted two of his sons with the responsibility of visiting every year the synagogue in the village of Derzs to inspect the condition of the building and the fence around it. "Make sure, my dear children," he wrote, "that the house where my dear parents and my great-great-grandparents lived and where I was born, along with my other brothers and one sister, may yet live for a long time to come, to the glory of God."

Yet another request followed: he asked two of his sons to go to Derzs, along with one of two rabbis he knew well, as soon as the seven days of deep mourning for him ended, and to have the rabbi ask forgiveness from Yankev's parents buried there that for his burial place he had chosen another cemetery instead of Derzs. The rabbi was to explain that Yankev wanted to be close to his own children, two of whom, along with his wife, were already buried on land he had acquired near his home in the village of Vaja.

In a gesture common in those days, he recommended to his sons that they each take a suit of his clothes and have it altered to fit them. His reasoning suggested that he understood well the peculiar small comforts of old age: his sons should wear his suits "so when they reach the age of seventy, it would make them feel good that they own a garment that was once worn by their father." He asked that the rest of his clothing be distributed among poor relatives and "worthy old people."

Yankev reserved his most eloquent words for an appeal to his children that they always observe the laws of Moses. The following call is underlined: "Live and conduct yourselves from now on the same way as you have done until now." He added: "At no time should you be ashamed that you are Jews and that you are honest Jews and that you are sincere Jews out of conviction. Besides keeping the laws at all times yourself, with all your heart and all your soul, you must raise your children so that they will do the same."

He left a large savings deposit so a substantial present could be given to each of his grandchildren when they married. According to his instructions, a bank official was to write a note along with the check: "Mazel tov from your loving grandfather, Yankev Schwarcz."

He advised against "too much mourning" after his death and completed the thought with sentences of singular serenity: "It was arranged by God that I was born the third child of my mother of blessed memory and that now I will be the third among my brothers who crosses the threshold to the other world. I ask you, my dear children, that you uncomplainingly submit yourselves to the Almighty's will. Because you are all the sweet fruits of a noble grapevine that was carefully selected and lovingly tended for a long, long time, you must try to keep the long-cherished refinements of those many years until the very end, and love and support one another in word and deed."

The final, tenth clause is subdivided into yet ten more subclauses, listing the items for which Yankev was grateful to God: "that He originated me from the good, dear parents

I had; that I could marry someone from the noble family that was my father-in-law's; that I leave behind noble and dear children that few other people in the world could be more proud of; that in all my life I was bedridden only twice, (because of typhus at age eighteen and because of a hornets' nest at age thirty-nine); that all my life I always had something to eat and to drink; that I always had respectable middle-class clothing; that I never had to be cold in the winter; that by God's grace I was permitted to reach this age (since my father of blessed memory only lived sixty-two years); and that all my life I was able to give charity to the poor."

At the end of the document, Yankev asked for forgiveness for his sins and transgressions, unspecified by him and unknown to those who knew him and whom I have known.

Was there really a man of such perfection? Could there have been? Could he have been made of one piece? No flaws, no contradictions? Might he have hidden from us a dark side of his personality? Was the precision he insisted on in his last will and testament obsessive? Did the dire threat of familial excommunication to anyone who prolonged a dispute over his last will conceal an angry, willful, vindictive tyrant?

Great-uncle Yankev must have had his imperfections and inconsistencies, but I can't point to any on the basis of what I have heard. As far as I can determine from conversations with people who knew him, he was the generous, God-fearing soul that the face value of his last will and testament shows him to be.

He was a giver, a category of man known as *nadav* in Hebrew. He is remembered as always bestowing presents and sending presents, and they were generous. His grandchildren recall that after he became ill with diabetes and took up residence in the county seat of Nyiregyháza to be near his doctor and the hospital, he travelled by train on the same day once a week to visit his estate in Vaja, whose management he had turned over to his son-in-law. While the train did not stop in another small village, Piricse, where some grand-children of his lived, they always waited for the train to pass because their grandfather would be at an open window, throw-ing candy and kisses.

For many years he provided monthly payments to his sister, Fanny, who was in financial trouble. After the Second World War, when one of his granddaughters, Ági, returned from Auschwitz and was without any funds, Fanny's son Endre gave her money with which to live and study at the university. When Ági thanked her cousin, Endre said: "Don't thank me. What I owe your grandfather is far more than what I can ever give you."

Yankev was lying in terrible pain in the hospital when he was told that one of his daughters had just given birth to a daughter, Ági. He was no longer able to speak, but those who saw him say the furrows on his brow eased, and he still had a smile on his face when he died a few hours later.

He was a powerful personality, the sort they called in his days "a man of iron." But unlike so many of them, he was at peace with himself and his world. He was convinced that living in a small, isolated village and cultivating the land was an ideal life, about as close to the Garden of Eden as possible since the Fall of Man, and he was determined not to let his children leave and succumb to the trivial attractions of city life or of the professions. To make sure that his children stayed in the countryside, he would not let them even finish high school, and he turned a deaf ear to a plea from one of his daughters—a brilliant student—to go to medical school. The force of his argument was such that one way or another, most of his children and grandchildren hung on to their rented land until the Second World War, when those who were not killed by the Nazis were driven out by the communists.

Like the rest of the family, Yankev believed in the importance of dreams. His children were not surprised that he kept appearing in their dreams after his death, usually to dispense practical advice concerning business opportunities and contracts.

One dream story has to do with his eldest son, Zoltán, who after serving as a lieutenant during the First World War began a business in Nyiregyháza leasing the fine agricultural machinery his father had bought. He rented out his best threshing machine to a rich man, but the machine sometimes worked and sometimes did not. The son, more of a gentleman than a businessman, was afraid to ask for the rental fee, and the rich man did not volunteer it. One night, Yankev appeared to Zoltán in a dream. "Son," he said, "go to that rich man and ask for the money. Don't ask for all the money because the machine didn't work all the time. But do ask for some of the money because the machine did work some of the time, and you are entitled to some compensation."

When Zoltán woke up in the morning, he told his wife about the dream, but decided against listening to his father for fear of angering the rich man. The following night Yankev again appeared to Zoltán. "You need the money, and that rich man has plenty of money," he said. "Go and ask him for the money."

Again Zoltán did nothing.

The third night, Yankev was angry and declared that he

would no longer appear in Zoltán's dreams if he didn't do what he must do. "I am done with you," Yankev warned. As Zoltán was having breakfast and talking the matter over with his wife, someone knocked on the door. It was the rich man, who had never before condescended to visit him.

"Here is your money for the rental of the threshing machine," the rich man said.

"Thank you," said Zoltán, astonished and embarrassed. "But you needn't have troubled to come here yourself—and so early in the morning. You must have more important things to do than coming here to pay me."

"Maybe I do," said the rich man. "But your father, whom I knew well when he was alive, appeared to me in my dream last night and reminded me that I owe you money and that I should pay you right away."

"But the machine didn't work all the time," said Zoltán, who discovered while counting the money that the rich man had paid him the entire fee.

"Look, my friend," the rich man said. "I can afford to pay you the full amount, thank God. But I can't afford to let your father get angry with me."

There was one dramatic difference between Great-uncle Yankev and my grandfather Karl. Yankev earned more money and managed a larger, more diversified estate producing far more items, such as honey, vegetables, and fruits, than his brother, who focused on wheat, tobacco, potatoes, and cattle. But instead of investing his profits in buying land, which to his brother Karl was "the sweetest and the most solid of all possessions," Yankev refused to buy the land he leased. He put his profits in the bank and gave much of his money away.

It was one thing to be modest, and the brothers agreed in

their dislike of ostentation. For instance, modesty prevented Yankev from moving into the imposing ancestral castle of Count Adam Vay, whose lands he leased and who offered to rent or sell his castle to Yankev. But apart from modesty, could it be that Yankev was afraid to show the world how prosperous he was? He might have argued with his brother Karl that leasing land was the prudent thing to do for someone who loved the land, which would not be inconsistent with the blessing conferred on the family by the Rabbi of Kálló, but that buying would mean being ensconced in the land as a new master and joining Hungary's proud historic elite, the landed gentry. While Karl felt secure and at ease, taking out loans to buy more and more land, Yankev was reserved and skeptical, having in mind all their forebears' experiences of discrimination and expulsions, and reminding himself that he was, relatively speaking, an upstart.

As a God-fearing Jew, Yankev felt the burden of responsibility for all of creation, which he saw teetering in a precarious balance between good and evil, rise and fall, triumph and defeat. He was aware that by reaching a wrong decision he would not only risk his own soul, but also the fate of his people, if not of humanity. How could he forget the many pages of the Talmud explaining the reasons for the fall of the Temple! A mistake in addressing an invitation to a wedding unleashed a chain of events in which the person invited in error and then humiliated by a disinvitation became an informer for the Romans against his own people, and he eventually helped to persuade the Romans to destroy the Temple.

Great-uncle Yankev helped to hold up a whole world as a Jew yoked to God, by a thousand silk cords of law and custom, yet at the same time he was anchored in the economics of everyday life. In that wholeness, every part had a meaning, and meaning was everything. He was equally at home in both worlds, the heaven above and the earth below, and he saw them as intertwined as two vines climbing the same post. He was a segment in a double helix of piety going back to Abraham, Isaac, and Jacob—and was closer to them than to his contemporaries.

Yankev's interest in grapevines was inspired as much by the biblical and talmudic references to the vineyard as a symbol of the Jewish people as by the fact that growing grapes was one of the most profitable, as well as one of the most complicated, ways to make use of even poor land. A cluster of grapes is a biblical figure of speech conveying a careful consideration of all issues, and wine, which is said to "gladden the spirit of man," stands for the sweetness of life. But a well-tended vineyard has also been the most valuable rural real estate. A vintner pruning his vines and organizing the complex operation of wine-making offers an extended biblical metaphor for the prudent, knowledgeable steward who deals with people and land "respectfully," as the traditional term puts it, or "caringly," as the contemporary idiom calls it.

The title page of a prayerbook for Rosh Hashanah and Yom Kippur, printed in Prague in 1800, used in one of the villages near Gyulaj, buried in a tin box in 1944 and found in the 1970s by someone digging up a yard.

10.

The Shot that Shattered
Rosh Hashanah

I have strange power of speech;
That moment that his face I see,
I know the man who must hear me;
To him my tale I teach.
COLERIDGE; *The Rime of the Ancient Mariner*

Some family stories are to be told again and again; others are to be blotted out from memory. Stories told across the dinner table or on a long journey, stories for children and for friends, for entertainment or instruction, are meant to be remembered and handed down, and perhaps even reenacted one day. But a family also has secrets not for sharing, and some can be so painful and sad that a decision is made that they are to be forgotten and never mentioned again.

Nevertheless, stories not for telling are still being told. That is because for one reason or another, someone who knows is prompted, sometimes even compelled, to pass them on.

One story that was not told in the Schwarcz family concerns the ninth and last child of my great-grandparents, a boy by the name of Moshe who was born deaf in the late 1860s. The Talmud, compiled some two thousand years ago, is stern: a deaf person who does not learn to speak has a status between a child and an imbecile, though a bit closer to a child. Such an individual is regarded as "not a responsible person" and "without an independent will," but he or she is allowed to marry, and a deaf Jew counts in the quorum of ten needed for communal prayer. But it is only in this century, with improved treatment of the deaf and improved possibility of communicating with them, that rabbis have removed the stigma of retardation.

The secret of Moshe's existence became known to my uncle Shumi when he was only six years old, in the early years of this century, and the person who revealed it was a tiny, soft-spoken, shriveled-up peasant woman in her late seventies, known to everyone as Grammy, even though, or perhaps because, she had no children. Everyone treated her with respect and affection, and she lived by herself in a little room of her own in the servants' quarters of the Schwarcz house-hold, though she was no longer expected to do any work. Many years ago, Shumi heard, she had been a nanny to Shumi's father, and that alone was reason enough for the family to care for her in her old age.

There were several other old retainers in the household of Róza and Karl Schwarcz who had few, if any, perceptible duties, but who were fed and clothed and paid wages because of some past merit. Little Shumi, the landowner's eldest son, chose Grammy as his special friend. He liked to spend time in her spotless, whitewashed room, where he was allowed to rummage through her battered wooden trunk that had once belonged to a soldier and was filled with treasures: colorful scarves favored by village women for presents; holy pictures in vivid reds, blues, and yellows sold at Greek Catholic pilgrimage spots; penknives with carved wooden handles, painted bright red, that he was allowed to open; heart-shaped, elaborately scrolled gingerbread mementoes of county fairs with little mirrors embedded in the hardened dough that he had to be careful not to break; a much-used little black prayer book; a collection of medicinal herbs she had gathered in the meadows that she used and prescribed for the people of the village.

But what mattered most to Shumi was that Grammy was the village storyteller, and Shumi was her most grateful audience. He loved to listen to stories, and he thought Grammy's stories were the best. Most of them were about people in the village of Gyulaj where they were both born and about the Schwarcz family, whose various enterprises and fondness for travel puzzled and fascinated the stolid, stay-at-home villagers.

One evening, as Grammy put Shumi to bed in the friendly, soft light of a kerosene lamp, she whispered to him that he was to hear a special story she had never told anyone else— a deep, deep secret, which he was not to tell anyone else, about an uncle he had never heard of.

His name was Moshe, but everyone called him by the nickname Mushika. He was deaf, born that way after his mother had given birth to eight robustly healthy children— seven sons and one daughter. Doctors examined Mushika, and they had his parents send him, while still a small child, to Vienna, more than three hundred miles away, which then had the best school in the world for teaching and sometimes curing the deaf. There it was soon discovered that Mushika was exceptionally intelligent and sensitive, which the family interpreted as the work of divine providence compensating him for his handicap. He was an outstanding student, particularly in mathematics, drawing, and painting. He was an avid reader of books in both Hungarian and German, and he wrote fine short stories and poems. His letters home were beautifully written and entertaining. Moreover, he was a lovable child.

Every year, Mushika came home for Rosh Hashanah, which the family turned into a birthday party for him, and life in the household revolved around making his stay at home happy. Everyone gave him presents and spent time with him. But neither his vocal chords nor his hearing could be developed, and he could only communicate in writing, on slips of paper. He tried to please everyone, but often looked sad and dejected.

By the time he turned eighteen, Mushika was a fine, handsome young man, Grammy remembered, and Rosh Hashanah that year was as festive as any earlier celebration. Everyone in the family and village was glad to see him. On the second night of the holy day dinner, after everyone had eaten a piece of challah dipped in honey and prayed that the new year be just as sweet, his parents, his brothers, and sister and other relatives and guests stayed for a long time at the dinner table to sing songs and talk. It was a large and noisy gathering, and no one paid attention when Mushika got up and left.

Then the night was shattered by a gunshot from the direction of the garden, and everyone rushed outdoors. Mushika's oldest brother found him under the lilac bushes. His face was covered with blood, his hands hung limp, and next to his body lay a revolver. By the time the doctor arrived, he was dead.

Grammy's explanation was not hard for little Shumi to understand: at age eighteen, Mushika was an adult, a sensitive and intelligent person, and he came to the conclusion during the joyful evening around the dinner table that he would never have a life like his brothers.

No one went to bed that night, Grammy said. Many servants wailed and cried. Mushika's parents and his brothers and sister paced back and forth in the house and in the garden, and weighed down with guilt, they wept as they talked about Mushika. It was the ordinariness of their lives—the chatter and the banter, the prayers and the songs—that drove the youngest brother to take his life. They could not feel his exclusion. He had lived in his world of silence, as if at the bottom of the sea, and they had not paid attention just when his attention was at its most acute.

According to Jewish law, suicide is "a lamentable waste of life." The strict rabbinical position is that a suicide denies God's sovereignty over the giving and the taking of life, and thus places himself or herself outside a God-fearing community, and ought to be buried without either ceremony and without the usual respect paid to the body. But lenient rabbis hold that a suicide should be neither punished nor honored, and that the body ought to be buried as simply as possible, with the minimum of ceremony.

Nevertheless, the Schwarcz family treated Mushika the way it treated any other of its dead. At dawn, Mushika's body was laid on the floor, and two lighted candles were placed by the head. Soon the men of the village burial society arrived, and they carefully washed the body. Then they lifted him up by his armpits and ankles, so his feet would not touch the ground, and threw water on his head to cleanse him of all earthly impurities. The women sewed a long white cotton shroud to cover his body, and a quorum of ten Jews, made up of his closest relatives, gathered to pray for Mushika's soul.

He was buried the following day in the family cemetery, and not just outside the fence where suicides are usually buried. His family observed the usual period of seven days' deep mourning. All mirrors in the house were covered, and there were prayers for his soul after each sunset.

There was one difference, however. On the headstone raised one year later, no name was incised. The white marble favored by the Schwarcz family was mute.

Grammy explained to Shumi that whether Jewish or Christian, ordinary people who commit suicide cannot be buried in the sanctified ground of a cemetery because he who rejects God's gift of life does not deserve the same consideration as he who dies when God chooses to take back that gift. Yet when it comes to the wealthy and the powerful, she added, they can change the law to suit their purposes or to reflect their feelings.

Did Grammy tell the story to Shumi to teach him about the differences between the poor and the rich at so early an age?

Perhaps. But it is at least equally likely that the suicide of a talented and likeable young man must have shocked her, and that she was angry that no one would talk about him, and that even his family treated him as if he had never lived. As a storyteller, Grammy could not stay silent—silence was inimical to her calling. As her life was drawing to a close, she felt she had to pass on the story to someone she was close to, someone who would listen and remember.

It was Shumi's decision to make friends with Grammy, the village storyteller, and that was one of his first independent acts. She was flattered because no matter how little, he was the young master.

The difference in class, though only vaguely if at all perceived by Shumi at such a tender age, only added to the drama of the story's transmission. She felt her power as keeper of the well of memories; in his thirst for stories, he also sensed her resentment. She knew she had gone too far in telling a forbidden family story, particularly to a child. But he was grateful for having been let in on a dark secret.

Grammy and Shumi are links in a chain of storytellers that reaches back to the first rememberers of tales who presided over the first fires tended by humans. In her own childhood in the early nineteenth century, Grammy must have listened to a storyteller, perhaps another childless old woman who kept alive the memory of men and women she had known or heard about. As for Shumi, he thought of Grammy as one of the storytellers who inspired him eventually to become the family chronicler.

In his sixties, Shumi recalled that he never asked to be told Mushika's story again, and that for many years he shuddered when reminded of the uncle he had never known.

11.
Half an Acre of Lace

> . . . Love is not love
> Which alters when it alteration finds,
> Or bends with the remover to remove:
> O no; it is an ever-fixed mark,
> That looks on tempests, and is never shaken;
> It is the star to every wandering bark. . . .
> SHAKESPEARE, *Sonnet CXVI*

In the 1970s the man who had been my grandmother Róza's landlord in Debrecen before the Second World War mailed to my uncle Shumi in Budapest a batch of family photographs. Perhaps the photos had been given to him for safekeeping before my grandmother and her eldest daughter, Elza, were deported to Auschwitz, or, just as likely, he had helped himself to whatever was left behind in the house. His name was Kovács, the stereotypical Hungarian name that means, and is as common in Hungary, as, Smith is in the English-speaking world.

A brooding, taciturn bachelor, Mr. Kovács was neither a friend nor an enemy. My mother, Anna, remembers him as a faceless little man who for nearly twenty years rang the bell on the first of the month to collect the rent.

After looking through the photographs, it becomes clear that he held on to at least one picture of each of Grandmother Róza's seven children, as well as of some other relatives. It appears that he was the secret keeper of our family tree. But why?

Many of the photographs show my red-haired aunt Elza, who in her youth in her native village of Gyulaj, some forty

Elza in Debrecen, in the early 1930s.

miles northeast of Debrecen, was often called the most beautiful woman in Szabolcs County. Educated in an exclusive
school run by nuns, she acquired the quietly assertive manners of Hungary's ruling class and the composure of a countess. According to her cousins, Elza was favored as her
parents' first child, and because she was the best student in
the family, particularly accomplished in speaking German,
she was frequently held up as a model for her sisters and
brothers. A devout synagogue-goer, Elza was closer to her
parents than to her brothers and sisters, who preferred not
to take part in rituals.

The poems she read in gold-embossed, leather-bound volumes, spoke of men who were either valiant or craven and
women who were either faithful or wanton, and regret followed
a fall from grace the way winter followed autumn. She mem-
orized ballads by József Kiss, the nineteenth century poet
who was from a village not far from hers and who turned the
fearful beauty of the Jewish faith into the heroic couplets of
traditional Hungarian poetry. In one poem often read at grad-
uation ceremonies in Jewish high schools, he described a Jew
living in a tottering thatched hut at the edge of a village who
devoted himself to the study of the mystical books of the
Kabbala. One by one, he loses his children: one is a soldier
shot through the heart in the revolution of 1848; another goes
to America, becomes wealthy, and marries a Christian; the
third becomes a great scientist who comes to reject God; and
the last, a daughter, runs away with a theatrical troupe. What
"the superficial world" considers a tragedy, the poet declares
a triumph of faith to be credited to "the iron pride of an
unbreakable father." In the last couplet, the old Jew remains
alone, but shares his seeming solitude with his God.

While Elza's father, a wealthy landowner, was still alive,

she turned down more than a dozen men who had proposed to her, and many more who were recommended by an itinerant matchmaker. She was looking for a perfect marriage with the man of her dreams and she refused to compromise because she knew she would find him, just as her parents had found each other.

The family's matchmaker was called Mr. Rezeda. He must have had a first name, but no one remembers anyone using it. He bore his family name with great pride. He might have chosen Rezeda himself, after the sonorous Hungarian word for a flower known as mignonette in English, beloved in Central European gardens for its exquisite fragrance. A tall, handsome, dignified gentleman who dressed fastidiously in black, he always carried with him a little leather-bound note-book containing the names, physical descriptions, and psy-chological profiles of many hundreds of eligible Jews in some ten counties of northeastern Hungary. Of great interest to him and his clients were the size and particulars of each woman's dowry, which was expected to provide the seed capital for a groom's business or professional practice. Mr. Rezeda dealt only with those wealthy enough to make his work worthwhile.

My grandparents' seven children and the scores of cousins living in close proximity made the Schwarcz clan a mainstay of his trade, and he was an honored guest at the dinner tables of all the Schwarcz patriarchs, who loved to discuss possible matches for their sons and daughters, nephews and nieces, including those still in diapers. "Now, let's just suppose," began a host as he invited Mr. Rezeda for an after-dinner stroll in the garden or, if the moon was out, along a tree-lined street, and in a conversation that stretched deep into the night, they proceeded to size up the character and the business of every Jew who owned or leased land within a hundred miles, because the family preference was for some-one who cultivated land. They also discussed the state of the world, for as a man who travelled throughout the year, Mr. Rezeda gathered all that was newsworthy. The matchmaker was elaborately courteous and astoundingly knowledgeable, and he was secure in the awareness of his invaluable service. He was as much a professional as a surgeon or a trial attorney.

My mother remembers how proud she was when around age thirteen, Mr. Rezeda, who had often joked with her while she was a little girl, first talked to her "seriously" as a potential client. He took some notes on what she had to say and solemnly promised to bring her a fine young man. She also claims that in the twenty or so years during which she had seen him at least twice a year, Mr. Rezeda did not seem to age. His full dark beard did not turn gray, his posture remained ramrod-straight, and he never seemed to tire of wandering through country roads, thinking of matches that his hosts might approve and heaven would bless.

After her father died and the family lost its wealth and moved to Debrecen, Hungary's second largest city, it was my mother's eldest brother, Shumi, who took charge of finding a suitable husband for Elza, his oldest sister. She was in her late twenties, and time was running out. Shumi introduced the beautiful Elza to an acquaintance of his, Feri Freifeld. One of the richest Jews in the county who also owned land, Feri was not known as the marrying type, and Mr. Rezeda, who had given up on him, advised the family against the choice. Feri was a man of the world irresistibly attracted to beautiful women, Gypsy music, and French champagne. He also had the fatal charm of the landed gentry and the looks of Adolphe Menjou, the matinee idol.

For both Elza and Feri, it was love at first sight. As was customary among Hungarian gentry, a class that lived on romance and fought a guerrilla war against reality, Feri sent her bouquets of flowers every day, and once a week dispatched a Gypsy band to play love songs under her window. The flowers were carefully cut to size and rearranged in vases through the small one-story house. The music was also appreciated, even if it was played around eleven o'clock, breaking the peace of a small-town street that went to bed at nine, if not earlier.

It would have been considered unforgivably philistine for the neighbors to complain about being awakened by Gypsy music; love had to be given its fair chance to disrupt the everyday. The songs were of romance leading to tragedy, and they were played in tremolo by at least two Gypsy violinists, accompanied by a cellist who deepened the chords of sorrow and longing. The lyrics were known to everyone, even while asleep, and men and women, young and old, dreamed sweeter dreams after the Gypsies had had their say and retreated once the chimes struck midnight.

Feri proposed, and even though Elza hesitated, uncertain whether such a union of opposites could work, her brother Shumi argued strongly and persuasively for the match, and Elza and Feri became engaged. She did not have a dowry, which was critical in those days, but Feri magnanimously dismissed as superfluous any thought of material gain on his part. "I am in love with the loveliest and most beautiful woman in the world," he declared. "No man could ask for more." At their wedding she was dressed in layers of white lace over white silk, which set off her red hair, the bronze favored by the Venetian master Titian. Feri, dark and dapper in top hat and tails, was the image of silky 1920s elegance.

A few weeks after the wedding, Feri suggested a visit to the theaters and night spots of Budapest. Elza was reluctant, saying that she needed time to settle in her new home on Feri's village estate by the river Tisza, and that she was not as yet ready to take on the capital. In that case, her husband said, he would go by himself. Elza thought he was joking or bluffing, but the following morning he caught the express to Budapest.

It was their first quarrel. Elza got out of bed, packed her clothes, ordered a carriage, and returned to her mother's house.

When Feri returned from Budapest a week later, Elza told him she wanted a divorce. Feri first laughed and then tried, with rising desperation, to talk her out of it, but she was adamant. To Elza, Feri had proved himself less than perfect, and she would not live with such a man. Her brother Shumi supported her, and in less than a year after they first met, Elza and Feri were divorced.

Although Jewish law and custom frowns upon any but the most inevitable social contact between a divorced man and woman who had no children, Feri continued to meet with his former wife. When Elza travelled to visit relatives in various cities, Feri often went there, too, supposedly on business and by chance, yet accompanying her to the theater or poetry readings and conducting himself as if still a member of the family. It was believed that on several occasions only the two of them met in Budapest, where lovers usually went to be lost in the metropolis. It would have been unthinkable for her sisters or female cousins to ask Elza to confirm or deny the gossip, and the men considered themselves above questions that might be interpreted as prying. "Elza lived her own

Aunt Elza in her parents' house in Gyulaj,
which she wished she had never left.

life," is what my mother says. "She was the aristocracy and the rest of us were the peasants. She could do as she pleased, but we were restricted every step of the way."

Two or three times a year, Feri visited Elza's mother's house for coffee and cakes and conversation. Either Elza's mother or my mother served as chaperone—after all, it would not have been proper to leave them alone—a role they all enjoyed because Feri was a most amusing raconteur and masterful in complimenting the ladies and praising the food they prepared.

A model of propriety, Elza sat up straight on her unpadded wooden chair, her back parallel with the straight back of the chair but never touching it. She would listen to Feri but avoid talking to him. She said little, no more than the minimum needed to be social. Her dark brown eyes were cast downward, often bathed in a fine mist of tears that no one was supposed to notice. Her focus was fixed on the lace that she was working on, as relentless as a spider—and just as solitary.

She was an accomplished and uncommonly fast lacemaker. Day after day, Elza wielded her steel crochet hook, looping tiny triangles and squares and rectangles, circles and semicircles and lozenges, which she arrayed in balanced clusters that swirled and flowed into one another with ease and grace. Working on her gardens of rosettes and stars, buds and leaves and tendrils, she never seemed to miss a stitch. But if she did make a mistake, she promptly undid the part, no matter how large, and began all over again. Often she designed the pattern even as she crocheted it. Her favorite shape was circular, and she finished even her rectangular tablecloths with an edging of semicircles.

In the forty-six years of her life—she started making lace when she was about ten—Elza might have completed close to half an acre of lace: collars and cuffs, fronts and borders for dresses and blouses; gloves extending to the wrist and gloves reaching the elbow; doilies for the backs and arms of armchairs, and for candlesticks, ashtrays, and porcelain figurines; coverlets for nightstands and commodes and dining tables; curtains for windows and French doors. Lace to be displayed in the house, lace to be folded and stored in capacious armoires and taken out once a year for airing, lace to be presented as gifts for relatives and for friends. In a family of storytellers, she was a woman of few words. The stories she told were spun out of cotton thread. But only she could decipher the characters, the plots, and the denouement.

Elza disliked housework and she did not seek employment outside. Well-organized and good with figures, she took charge of the house and the family budget. She collected the salaries of her brothers and sisters and handed out their spending money according to a scale she designed and everyone accepted, albeit with an occasional grumble. For instance, Elza's clothing was sewn by one of the best seamstresses in town, and sometimes even in Budapest, but her sisters had to accept less expensive arrangements. Her explanation was that she made do with fewer pieces of clothing than her fashion-conscious sisters.

Another grievance against Elza, going back to the days in Gyulaj, was that because she was in control of all incoming mail, she knew of every letter received by her brothers and sisters as well as any cousins who happened to stay in the house, yet no one was permitted to know about any of her correspondence, which was believed to be copious. She was often seen composing long letters.

Elza told the one servant what to cook and where to get the ingredients. She was a frugal comptroller who took pride in getting a bargain at the poultry market, usually by announcing the price she was willing to pay and not accepting compromises, while the servant standing behind her waited with the wicker baskets.

Elza insisted on drawing social distinctions that her "modern" relatives thought outdated. Visiting in Huszt, a town high in the pine forests of the Carpathian mountains, Elza was surprised to note that her stylish young cousin, whose father owned the local sawmill, was on a first-name basis with the ragged-looking son of a mechanic. "You have to know who you are," she chided the cousin. "We are both Jews and we are both young," the cousin shrugged.

While she did not cook any meals, the sauerkraut and pickled cucumbers and green tomatoes she prepared were the best in the family. "In Elza's hands, vegetables turned sour amazingly fast," says my mother, an expert in baking sweets, who suggests that "Elza's special gift had to do with her personality." This is as far as my mother will go in saying something truly negative about Elza, born ten years before she. "Elza was severe with us, her younger sisters and brothers," she adds, "far more severe than our mother. We were all afraid of her."

It has been said in the family that Elza loved but once, and there was also a consensus that one day Feri would give up his life of wine, women, and song, and return to Elza for good, though neither of them ever said anything specific that would have given weight to such an expectation.

The lesson that a cousin some twenty years younger than Elza remembers learning from her was from an otherwise lighthearted conversation about unrequited love. "Is there any other?" Elza had asked, in a matter-of-fact tone that expected no answer.

198

She had a wooden box, the size of a thick dictionary, which she always kept in her room under lock and key, in her armoire. Its contents were a deep secret. The family knew that she had kept a diary from her childhood on, and they assumed she hid it in the wooden box, perhaps along with other things of special value to her. No one was ever allowed to look inside the box, let alone glimpse even the cover of her diary.

From time to time my mother tried to coax Elza into disclosing the contents of the box, but Elza barely deigned to answer "No," and the key was always with her, together with all the keys to the pantry, the cupboard, and the cellar.

The one photograph that shows Elza the way she liked to be seen was taken when she was about eighteen. She is leaning out of a window artfully framed by a flowering vine that climbs up her father's house, the house where she was born and, as her sisters would add, over which she reigned and which she wished she had never left.

Because so many of the photographs returned by Mr. Kovács, the landlord, show Elza, and because he seems to have discarded extra photographs of many other family members, one can't help but wonder about his fascination with her. Could he have been secretly in love with Elza? Perhaps he was, but it would have been from far, far away, because Elza is most unlikely to have condescended even to talk to him. As for the large number of photographs showing Elza, it might have had to do with the fact that she was the most frequently photographed member of the family, the favorite model of her brother Mishi, an amateur photographer.

The letter from Mr. Kovács accompanying the photographs, neatly packed in a shoebox, asked for Shumi's help in a lawsuit. But knowing my uncle, Mr. Kovács should have been

Elza in a photograph she sent
to her cousin Jenny.

certain that Shumi would have helped in any case. Besides, few people would keep someone else's family pictures for three decades in the expectation that returning them might secure a favor.

We will never know Mr. Kovács's purpose. He died soon after he sent his gift, if gift is the right word. There is always the possibility that he was given other family mementoes for safekeeping as well. We do not know because no relative whom my grandmother might have told such a detail survived the war, so no claim could be made.

On June 29, 1944, Elza and her mother, along with thousands of other Jews from Debrecen, were herded into cattle cars. After three days they arrived at the railroad station in the then unknown Polish village of Auschwitz. A Nazi officer looked them over to decide who was strong enough to be sent to work and who should be gassed immediately. He dispatched Elza, a vigorous woman in her forties, in one direction and her frail, elderly mother in the other. According to a surviving relative who witnessed it, Elza explained to the officer in her flawless German that she would not leave her mother. The German shrugged. "Do what you want," he told her.

Sometime earlier, a guard had ordered Elza to hand over the wooden box that she held under her arm. When she refused, the guard struck her in the face and took it away.

Feri found himself in the same transport with Elza and died with her in the same gas chamber.

In an outdoor restaurant in the town of Nyiregyháza in the
early 1920s, Uncle Mishi (to the right, seated) and a friend
listen to two Gypsy violinists.

12.
The Loves of a Rose Gardener

How long do the merits of the fathers endure?
THE TALMUD

When my mother visited me in Paris in 1966, she brought with her the telephone number of a friend she had not seen for nearly fifty years. Her name was Mantzi, and she was my mother's age, born in the first years of our century in the small town of Nyirbátor, some ten miles from my mother's native village of Gyulaj. When they first met, in their teens, Mantzi's father owned a little grocery store and made a modest living, and my mother's father was an important landowner, though his estate was on the verge of bankruptcy.

My mother told me that in her youth, around 1920, Mantzi, pretty and pushy, "used to her advantage the unusual quality of her eyes, which had the admittedly intriguing color of violets," in an attempt to "snare" Mishi, the most handsome of my mother's four brothers. Mishi, however, was interested in romance, not marriage, and in any case his family did not think that the daughter of a grocer, albeit a devout Jew, was good enough for Mishi. My mother does not deny that she was pleased when Mantzi's plans came to naught. Ambitious and restless, Mantzi emigrated to France sometime in the late 1920s, and the only information my family had about her was that she became a seamstress.

My mother telephoned Mantzi, who suggested that we meet for tea at her favorite place in the French capital, the Café de l'Opera.

"But how will we recognize each other?" my mother asked.

"The color of my eyes hasn't changed," Mantzi said. "And I think you still remember that color."

"I do," my mother said. "But it so happens that my son is the very image of my brother Mishi in his youth. You will be able to recognize him instantly."

My mother thought it would be impolite to arrive in the café one minute late, so we got there fifteen minutes early. Mantzi was already there, wearing immaculate white gloves, a jaunty white hat, and a tailored blue jacket. Her eyes were indeed a rare shade of violet.

My mother wore a smart gray suit and a string of pearls, elegant in an understated sort of way.

Mantzi didn't waste a minute in briefing us about her family. Her husband, "a sweet man," was a prominent, wealthy jeweler and highly respected in the Paris Jewish community, where he was quite active. Their daughter, "a true beauty," had married the scion of one of France's oldest and finest families. Their son, "a very smart lawyer" who had just completed his studies, already had a job in the best law firm in Paris but was not yet ready to get married.

At times, Mantzi spoke a bit too loud, and on one occasion she tugged at my mother's sleeve to emphasize a point. My mother carefully straightened the sleeve.

Usually talkative and friendly, my mother behaved with a great deal of reserve while sipping her tea. To a passerby, she might have appeared a regular customer in France's classiest café, across the street from the Opera.

But the glittering establishment of marble and etched glass

·

204

was wholly incidental. Within no more than ten minutes, half a century peeled away, and two world wars, expropriations, deportations, and revolutions unhappened. Once again, Mantzi was the grocer's daughter, and my mother, the landowner's. Mantzi was as common as if she still helped her father pour potatoes out of their sacks and into their bins, and my mother was as serenely dignified as an heiress from the ranks of landed gentry engaged in polite conversation.

"How is your brother Mishi?" Mantzi asked my mother. "What kind of woman did he marry? Does he have children?"

"Oh, he is fine, thank you," my mother replied in a tense, controlled tone. "But, unfortunately, his wife is not well just now. We are not getting any younger, you know." She added as a kind of afterthought that Mishi had no children.

Mantzi asked if by any chance my mother might have a family photograph with her. She did.

Mantzi pulled out of her handbag a pair of glasses.

My mother identified her brothers and sister, and Mantzi slowly and wordlessly scrutinized every member of the family. Finally, Mantzi announced in a flat voice: "I wouldn't recognize your brother Mishi if he sat across the table from me."

Then Mantzi put down the photograph and looked at me through her thick lenses for the first time.

"My God," she said, "you do look like your uncle! What incredible family resemblance! But—and I do hope that you don't mind my saying so—he was much more handsome than you are. He was the most handsome man I have ever known. Also the best company."

She took off her white gloves and held my hand. "Believe me, I have a fine husband who brings home every franc he makes," she said. "He works hard and he is good to me. But your uncle Mishi did not marry the right person. I know.

Don't try to tell me otherwise. I even know that his wife's eyes don't match: one eye is brown, the other is green. There is a superstition that people with eyes that don't match are not to be trusted. In her case, that superstition is right on the mark. Besides, she couldn't have any children. Right?"

There was a pause. My mother and I looked at each other, astonished. How did Mantzi know all this? Who could have kept her au courant? To this day, we don't know.

It took at least a minute before my mother composed herself and said, with a deep sigh: "You are right on all counts."

"I would have made a good wife to your brother Mishi," Mantzi said to my mother. "And I would have been a good aunt to you," she said to me.

She took off her glasses, and her eyes were filled with tears.

"You have lovely eyes, Aunt Mantzi," I said, and I knew— I *knew*—that I was repeating words from another time, another place, another person: "The color of violets in the rain."

Her hand pressed mine so hard that it hurt.

Oh, my beloved Uncle Mishi! The family's darling, a dapper bon vivant, a fixture in the noisiest coffeehouses of the land!

With a fragrant white carnation in the buttonhole of his well-cut jacket, Mishi was never so broke that he couldn't afford one red rosebud for a date.

A second son, Mishi inherited his father's congeniality and optimism in their entirety. He was well liked in the village of Gyulaj, where he was born, and then in the cities of Debrecen and Budapest, where he spent his adult life. Women were attracted by his manners and wit, by his full head of raven-black, wavy hair, and by his dark brown eyes

Clockwise, from the top: Uncle Mishi as a man-about-town in his twenties; a soldier on the Russian front in the Second World War; a prosperous businessman in the 1950s; as a retiree in the late 1960s.

that sparkled. "Our father's eyes," his sisters always said, with pride. "The eyes of a snake charmer," other women added, with admiration.

His father's repeated and increasingly desperate attempts to make him learn a bit of Talmud and to have him observe the laws of Moses rolled off of him. At least keep the fast on Yom Kippur, his father finally pleaded, and in his last will and testament implored his two oldest sons only to remember his last words: "There is a God!"

But Mishi, whose Hebrew name was Moshe—for Moses— paid no attention. He was not a rebel, and between him and his father there were never any scenes, nor harsh words. And he never converted. His slipping out from behind the ramparts of the faith was undramatic and guiltless. His version of a talmudic academy was a sharp debate about the talents of a politician or an actress, to be fought across his favorite table, by the window, in the coffeehouse where he spent much of his time. The code he followed—faithfully—was that of the landed gentry. The fact that his family had lost its lands while he was in his early twenties only added irony to the charm of his observance.

Between the two world wars there were many Hungarians who suffered a similar decline of their fortunes and who liked to draw parallels between their lives and the nation's fate: after the First World War, under the aegis of Wilsonian self-determination and France's insistence on revenge, Hungary lost two thirds of its territory to its neighbors, and found itself outnumbered and outgunned by them. The neighbors also happened to be hereditary enemies. Some Hungarian patriots went into mourning, and many could never recover from the shock. But much of the landed gentry, which still set the tone in society, pretended that nothing had changed. "What matters is good manners," declared triumphantly a song in one of the popular operettas of the time. "Time cannot rush me."

"Bastard time!" Mishi would mutter, and he was determined to live as if he were still the son of a wealthy father. He conducted himself as if he were still the citizen of the prewar kingdom—what he and many others affectionately called "The Happy Hungary." With a wink in his eyes and a thousand and one stories on the tip of his tongue, Mishi carried the torch for a defeated class in a defeated country.

He was a good horseman and a nimble-footed dancer of waltzes. Watching him take off his hat, invariably set at a rakish angle, and kiss a lady's hand was theater, and one could only applaud his performance.

He could enter some half a dozen restaurants and the Gypsy violinists on stage would promptly recognize him and strike up his favorite song, a lively tune titled "I Was Born in a Rosebush." On the rare occasions when he had money, he smoked good cigars. Otherwise, he sucked on a pipe with the equanimity of an oriental potentate, or he made a bit of a show out of lighting a cigarette and blowing wreaths of smoke toward an indifferent ceiling.

He both won and lost large amounts of money playing gin rummy and the horses. But one couldn't tell by looking his smiling face how he had fared.

From his early twenties on, he had the same dozen or so chums, with whom he would stay up until dawn in an outdoor restaurant or in a smoke-filled coffeehouse, drinking coffee and swapping jokes and anecdotes about politics and personalities. They called themselves the Tin-Ear Choir, and it was a noisy, rowdy bunch of journalists and artists, rumpled bohemians and unemployed aristocrats. Mishi wouldn't let his two younger sisters date any of them—oh, how my mother complained about those double standards!—but some of them did show up in the house in Debrecen and adopted Mishi's saintly yet tolerant mother, Róza, as their mother-confessor.

Even though his mother shed many a tear over Mishi's life-style, he was also the one who could make her laugh. "Whenever he was home, he brought warmth and cheer to the house," his older brother Shumi wrote in his memoirs.

Mishi always knew the latest jokes, and he was ready with the finest old stories to illustrate a point. Or he told an old story for the sake of "telling a good story that had not been told for a long time yet deserved to; because if not told, the story might be, God forbid, forgotten one day soon."

Beginning with his days in high school in the county cap-ital, Nyiregyháza, Mishi was fascinated with the theater. Among his girlfriends he had chorus girls and actresses, jaded prima donnas, ambitious walk-ons and aspiring intellectuals. He could be most positive—and sympathetically analytical—when a woman friend switched from long tresses to a short, boyish "French" haircut. "Don't you have any second thoughts, don't you regret it," Mishi said, and he was most persuasive. He weighed with all the seriousness of a presiding judge the color and the cut of a dress he decided were the most flattering to a date. He swept former girlfriends off their feet by keeping, for years and years, mementoes such as a playbill, a dinner menu, or a ribbon that had been part of an elaborate nightdress. He reduced them to tears by re-membering their parting words—and expressing his regret at not having responded to those words more effectively. Old flames liked to meet with him, for a cup of coffee or for a hurried chat on a street corner, and the long-ago affair ap-peared a bit more memorable every time they saw him.

He loved all that was fleeting and illusory, all that sweetened, perfumed, or veiled reality, even if for only one short, deceptive moment.

With the ease of a swallow zigzagging in flight, he fell in love with all kinds of women: a big, motherly blonde who daydreamed all day long and wore an ivory cross on a long golden chain; a wiry little tap dancer who lost her temper easily and who begged him to accompany her to the synagogue where she wanted to pray for her father's soul; a tall statuesque countess who wore her gowns as if she were in attendance to the Empress Elisabeth, Franz Josef's wife; and a modest little chambermaid who had little to say that was not an apology for her having made yet another social gaffe.

One girlfriend was proud of her slender waist and thought that she pleased him by keeping herself fashionably slim; another could not resist chocolates and was certain that he did not mind her putting on a little weight so she looked like "a traditional woman." He courted each one of them as if no other female existed in the world, and he held no grudges if they left him for someone else, or if they had enough of his contempt for the institution of marriage, or if they got fed up with his objections to turning the relationship "permanent" or "serious."

He called young girls "seedlings," and he classified mature women as wildflowers of the countryside or peonies of an urban courtyard, as lush poppies or refined tea roses. He liked to go out for long walks in early summer, when women paraded their new dresses in the fresh wind. He admired well-shaped legs and would follow, from a respectable distance, for as long as a mile a particularly good example, and he examined the tracks they made in the snow as if he was conducting a scientific experiment.

211

Speaking of the women he courted, he would sometimes call them by the perfume they used, such as lily of the valley or Chanel No. 5. If someone applied a particularly strong perfume or a lot of it, Mishi would say, "She smells like a harem girl," and wink approvingly.

He sent bouquets of roses to the women he courted, or he presented at least one single, symbolic, superior rosebud. The roses he offered were always red, the color of passionate love.

It did not bother Mishi that until after the Second World War—for more than twenty-five years of his adult life—he did not have a steady, regular job or an apartment he could call his own. On the contrary, he thought of the period between the two world wars as his own golden age. He loved being footloose, spending all that he earned as a travelling salesman selling coffee beans and the little hand-operated mills that ground the beans, as a representative for an advertising agency, as a photographer and as a journalist for an anti-Nazi news service. He went from job to job, somehow managing to stay afloat and not look worried.

He believed that prosperity—or at least a source of steady income—was just around the corner. He also kept making—and losing—bets to the effect that Hitler would not be able to conquer yet another country. Mishi was certain that Churchill or Roosevelt, and particularly the combination of the two, would outsmart Stalin.

Looking back, he called the Second World War "the jamboree."

During both world wars he was amazingly, astoundingly lucky. In the first, he would have been drafted at the end of the year Hungary quit the war. In the second, thanks to his many friends and connections, he was conscripted as a chauffeur in the Hungarian army, while other able-bodied Jewish males between the ages of eighteen and fifty-five were required to do forced labor that was often far worse than being at the front. The captain he ended up driving across Russia turned out to be a younger brother of a friend of Mishi's father, and the captain served in the important post of liaison officer between the Hungarian and German armies on the Russian front.

Nobody bothered to look into Mishi's identity papers—which were forged; the family name was listed as Szemes instead of Schwarcz—primarily because it was impossible and unthinkable for a Jew to be assigned to such a position of trust. It did not occur to anyone to check his birth certificate because he handled himself with such congenial aplomb—the gentry's version of chutzpah.

He was found out toward the end of the war during a routine examination of identity papers. People were shot for far less, yet Mishi was simply sent off to a forced-labor camp in western Hungary. After the Germans withdrew to Austria and the camp's guards fled, Mishi walked some hundred and fifty miles to Budapest. I remember seeing him enter through the gate of my aunt's garden. He walked with his usual bouncy stride—as if he had just come from an outing, a stroll, a date.

A few weeks later he returned to Antzi, a former girlfriend who had left him at the beginning of the war for an army officer later killed in Russia. Antzi was a village woman who worked her way up in Debrecen and became a manicurist and a photographer's model. In the kind of coincidence that one tends to dismiss as romantic overdose in novels by Dumas and Dickens, her grandmother happened to be the sister of the young Christian maid whom the Jews of Tiszaeszlár were accused of killing in 1882 in a ritual murder, but who in fact drowned in the river Tisza. And it had been Mishi's grandfather Samuel who took the initiative to raise the funds for defending the Jews who were eventually acquitted.

My mother and her sister talked Mishi into marrying Antzi, then in her early thirties, in 1946. They argued that as he was in his early forties, he needed to settle down in a stable marriage, save money for respectable living quarters, and acquire a steady job.

Mishi took over—and paid such a low price that it was practically an inheritance—a tire repair shop in downtown Budapest. The owner was a friend from the forced-labor camp who reached the conclusion in 1946 that the communists would soon take over Hungary and nationalize everything, so he fled across the border to Austria and then emigrated to Argentina. Originally, the friend tried to talk Mishi into joining him, but Mishi, then active in the Smallholders' Party, which was opposed to the communists, was convinced that his friend was paranoid. Besides, Mishi refused to consider leaving Hungary, the land of his birth and his forebears. He had left Hungarian territory only once in his life, and then because he had to.

In about a year, the communists did start taking over the government and began expropriating first large and then small businesses. Mishi was saved by a stroke of luck that many in the family and outside it as well thought was nothing short of miraculous.

One lovely sunny spring afternoon, Mishi was sitting in a garden chair outside his shop. Puffing on his pipe and wearing a newly pressed, conservatively cut pearl-gray suit—his favorite color for a suit—he appeared the image of comfort and contentment. As he was surveying the passing show and waiting for his friends to drop by, a Soviet military truck stopped in front of him. An army major got out and addressed him in a strange language.

Mishi exhausted his knowledge of Russian by saying that he did not understand a word. Then the major switched to German, which was the only foreign language Mishi could speak, a little, from his childhood when his father had forced him to study it as the language of the empire.

It turned out that the major was an Armenian who stopped his truck because he caught a glimpse of Mishi and took him for a fellow Armenian on account of his olive skin, aquiline nose, and dark hair. "Sitting in that chair, you looked like a pasha, and like one of my own," the Armenian told him.

Mishi laughed and said that he thought the mistake was a compliment because he was not as smart as an Armenian, and he somehow managed to tell a joke in his broken German about an Armenian, a Jew, and a Turk, which showed that the Armenian could easily outwit the other two. The joke made the Armenian laugh. Then Mishi invited the Armenian to taste his specialty—his version of Turkish coffee—and told his favorite story about coffee, again in his broken, primitive German:

In the best coffeehouse in heaven, the menu lists many different kinds of coffee: with cinnamon and with chocolate, with cardamom and with whipped cream, with brandy and with chicory. Each concoction has its own fancy name and fancy price. However, *"aber ein Kafé"*—but just coffee—is the cheapest, the plainest, and the best item on the menu, and, for a connoisseur such as the Lord Himself, that is the only coffee to order.

The Armenian liked Mishi's little anecdote, liked Mishi's coffee, and liked Mishi. He told Mishi that he had on his truck some twenty top-quality, brand-new radios of the famous brand Minerva, direct from the German Reich, which he personally had "liberated" from the factory where they were made, and he wanted to sell them to Mishi. Mishi said he had no money to buy such things, and besides he was afraid he would be caught and jailed for selling contraband.

The Armenian said that Mishi could have the radios on consignment and pay for them whenever they were all sold, however long that took. He was not in a hurry. As for Mishi's fears of arrest, he would see to it that a friend of his—and he had good connections—turned Mishi's shop into a Soviet state company. "Then no one from the Hungarian government will ever dare to enter your shop," the Armenian said.

After a little more hesitation, Mishi went along with both suggestions. "Really, what else could I do?" he later defended himself to his family. "The Armenian was pleasant and seemed honest. What more can you ask for? Besides, I used up all my German words and the effort of speaking a foreign language exhausted me."

The next day, the Armenian's friend showed up and had Mishi sign some documents which turned the shop into a Soviet company.

In the years that followed, Mishi's tire repair shop, registered as a Soviet company with Mishi as its manager, was given a wide berth by the People's Republic of Hungary and its all-powerful Secret Police. Not only was the shop permanently saved from the nationwide, no-exemptions-granted expropriation program—which would have meant Mishi's immediate dismissal—but for the first time in his life Mishi earned good money, and this at a time when all his relatives and friends were struggling to make ends meet.

In the office in the back of his shop, Mishi felt safe enough to hold court every day. He made coffee and entertained his friends, many of them from the landed gentry of Szabolcs County, every one of them an enemy of the communist regime. They traded the latest rumors about arrests and conspiracy trials and other features of life under Stalin, the Great Father of Peace-Loving Humanity, and they debated whether there was really some truth to the regime's charges of anti-communist plots.

Soviet army officers had a well-deserved reputation for pillaging and raping, and for treating Hungary as enemy territory. Very few Hungarians would have given a friendly reception to a Soviet officer dropping in on them. Like most Hungarians, Mishi looked at the Red Army as a hostile army of occupation, and yet, somehow, for some reason he could never explain, Mishi was able to see a guest in the major who wore the red star on his cap, and that hospitality made all the difference.

In a world that is whole, one good deed invokes another— just as on a healthy tree, a branch buds out and grows in strength to balance another branch. A secret symmetry aligned the Armenian major of the Russian army, responsible for Mishi's good fortune after the Second World War, with the Russian prisoners-of-war of the First World War who were greeted, fed, and employed by Mishi's father three decades earlier. The seemingly chance encounter of Mishi and the major on the Budapest asphalt sprouted from seeds sown in the Gyulaj sand. For on a moral ledger, the credit earned by a father's generosity may be paid back to a son.

Mishi would have smiled at the talmudic notion of a moral ledger as too serious for his taste. But as an inveterate spinner of yarns who could fall in love with a pretty phrase, he would have been delighted to accept a metaphor speaking of his cashing in his father's chips in a bazaar of favors and kindnesses.

Based in Vienna, across the minefields and electrified fences wires of the Iron Curtain, the Armenian visited Mishi several times, bringing luxury items unavailable in Hungary such as real chocolates and Brazilian coffee beans, nylon stockings and chewing gum. Mishi insisted on paying for the items he bought for himself and his family, and he found a friend to sell the rest.

From time to time, his employees did have to take care of flat tires on Soviet vehicles, but the Hungarian People's Republic and its secret police paid no attention when the shop earned money fixing the tires of other customers. The business thrived.

Uncle Mishi and Aunt Antzi bought a plot of land in a village, just outside Budapest, called Remete, a word which means "hermit" in Hungarian. They built a small, simple one-story house with two rooms, a kitchen, and a bathroom— and yet another room was supposed to be added after Antzi had a child.

Mishi got up at five in the morning to board the bus going to the city, and he left his shop at exactly four-thirty to catch the bus home. It took him as much as four hours a day to commute, but, he said, living in Remete made it all worthwhile. The bus he had to transfer to in the outskirts of Budapest was always late, and he boasted when he "beat the bus" and saved the fare by walking the last two miles home. "Walking is one of the best things in the world," he said.

His pace was unhurried, having little in common with the purposeful march of one whose mind focuses on getting somewhere and who worries about being late. Nor did he walk slow and weary like those whose trudging suggests they are resigned to going home or to the workplace or to the nearest tavern. Mishi had the confident, bouncy, steady stride of an explorer who looks forward to the next bend of the road. He walked the way the pious pray: as if nothing else in the world mattered.

He started a vegetable patch and a flower garden, raised geese and chickens, and planted fruit trees. The barnyard was separated from the garden by a thick hedge of lilacs, just as it had been on his parents' estate.

The family encouraged him: he said his ambition was to bring back a bit of the glory that was Gyulaj.

Antzi stayed at home, to take care of the house and the garden. But she said she did not like to dirty her hands, and even though she was born in a village she could not be expected to like living in another village for the rest of her life, certainly not after her years as a city person in Debrecen. She sabotaged some of Mishi's projects—for instance, she said she hated geese and she eventually got rid of them. Mishi did most of the work in the kitchen garden and said that he loved it.

Mishi insisted that he did not miss his footloose days— not at all. He said he had tired of the city where buildings and pavements, people's faces and office interiors, had "the color of wet ashes—and often smelled worse." He was ready to follow in his parents' footsteps, he declared. In the village of Remete he was "getting back home to the blessed color green."

He acquired a black puppy—a mutt because he believed mutts were the best and black because he thought that was the best color for a dog—and he trained him and talked to him as if to a child. The dog was named Matyi—the nickname of the Hungarian communist dictator Mátyás Rákosi—which was not a prudent thing to do because someone could have reported him to the authorities, and people in those days were given a year or two in jail for making fun of The Leader. At times, when he felt devilish, Mishi picked a crowded coffeehouse or a bus to say to a friend in a loud voice, "That damned stinking Matyi chewed up my socks" and then watched with amusement how people chuckled, or looked around nervously, and how some moved a few steps away.

A friendly dog who played soccer with children and loved every member of the family, Matyi was also an active male who was never chained, and he roamed through the village at night. Mishi took great pride in Matyi's amorous pursuits, and the entire family had to hear whenever Matyi returned home "from the field of love and honor" with an ear in tatters or with yet another gash on his ribs.

The story Mishi loved to tell starred a splendid white purebred sheepdog, a prize-winning specimen of the Hungarian breed called komondor. She was twice the size of Matyi, and her owner, planning to breed her, built a six-foot-high stockade fence to protect her from mutts such as Matyi. But on one occasion, Matyi or the sheepdog chewed a hole through the fence, and in due time she gave birth to two puppies, one white and one black, both of which looked just like Matyi.

Soon after that event, which Mishi duly reported to his family, there was a torrential rain that flooded the sheepdog's house. As unusual as it may seem, she brought her puppies over to Matyi's house, which, built on a concrete slab, remained dry, and she took up residence there. Though most dogs would fight to keep out another dog, Matyi accepted the arrangement—"What a gentleman!" Mishi said—and slept at the entrance of his house and played with the puppies.

"I raised a good father," Mishi said with pride. After the sheepdog weaned her puppies, she returned home. But Mishi kept the black, male puppy, a replica of Matyi in every way.

From the beginning, the house in Remete was troubled by moisture. No architect, no engineer, not one of the many jack-of-all-trades and blue-collar know-it-alls Mishi brought to the house for consultation could find a solution. No amount of insulation helped; even a new foundation did not do the job. Somehow, moisture seeped into the walls insidiously, made the paint flake off even the ceiling, and destabilized the plaster, which first looked as if it had a rash and then started to crumble. Even in the summer the rooms felt cold and clammy and smelled musty. And the foundation for the third room, a concrete parapet nearly one foot above the ground, reminded everyone that the hoped-for child had not arrived.

Once lively and cheerful, Antzi turned sour. On occasion she confided to a relative that her low mood was because yet another doctor had told her she had virtually no chance of bearing a child.

Even before her marriage she was a secret drinker, and as the years passed she drank more and more, and with less and less secrecy. In her youth she had fine, sharply chiseled features which the alcohol and her unhappiness—and who can tell which came first?—dissolved little by little into puffy, doughy confusion.

Mishi never complained and he put up a brave front. His sisters and sisters-in-law thought that his silence on the subject of his wife's drinking only added to his suffering, but his brothers and brothers-in-law tended to believe that he did the right, manly thing in keeping his problems to himself.

Nevertheless, if anyone in the family or among his friends had a problem, Mishi was the man to turn to. He was always sympathetic and helpful, and he had a way of letting others think that they thought of his idea for a solution first.

On Sundays throughout spring and summer, he entertained his family and his friends on a spacious patio. He served fresh fruit picked from his trees, and compote and preserves made from those fruits—the work of my mother Anna. He had a favorite tree that bore fragrant apricots the size of large peaches. At first their color was ivory which then turned a French Impressionist's mix of soft yellow and fleshy pink, with unexpected streaks of scarlet. Mishi liked to describe his apricots as having "the flavor of Gyulaj."

And, of course, he made his special coffee. He kept the coffee beans in a battered tin box he had had since his youth, and he roasted them on a heavy cast-iron skillet that was never used for any other purpose. He then ground up the beans in an old wooden brass-fitted hand-mill. He turned the handle slowly—or as an honor, a young nephew was asked to perform the job under his supervision. But no one under the age of eighteen was permitted to taste the strong, fragrant brew which he served in antique Viennese porcelain of blue and gold, with amorous shepherds and shepherdesses painted on the sides of the cups. They rested on a silver tray with a dainty, playful ribbon running all around the edge.

Except for whatever was connected with coffee, Mishi extolled simplicity. For instance, he seldom wore anything other than a solid tie, usually dark blue or bright red. His favorite food was bean soup, with whatever meat happened to be available. "Eat the food of the poor and work for the rich," he would quote the old Turkish proverb. And bean soup was just about the only dish Antzi prepared for the family.

Dinner was held around a circular barbecue pit, crafted out of local fieldstone, where as many as ten people could squeeze together, with ample room for their legs in the trench around the pit. It was the kind of feast customary among Hungarian herdsmen out in the fields and hunters roughing it in the woods. In the sudden chill that descended after sunset even during the summer, the blaze in the center felt just right, and the glowing embers were lovely in the darkness.

Mishi gave everyone a sturdy three-foot-long branch he had cut from the wild growths of the black locust trees that sprouted in ditches throughout the village of Remete. He sharpened one end, which speared a chunk of bacon, cut through to the skin at the bottom in a kind of a grid, which was to be roasted slowly over the flames. When the fat started to drip, one removed the stick from the fire and held the bacon over a hefty slice of bread covered with onion—in rings or all chopped up. Once the hot fat saturated—and toasted— the bread, it was ready to eat. In the end, the bacon was crisp, and it too was eaten with more bread and more onions. All the onions were freshly dug up from the vegetable patch, and the bread was the crusty, thick bread of the countryside, often made by my mother who did not mind in the least getting up early in the morning to begin baking. Mishi's eyes sparkled when he praised her bread—and that was the applause my mother looked for.

Uncle Mishi greeted each guest as if he had not seen him or her for years, and when saying good-bye, he accompanied everyone at least as far as the gate, some three hundred feet from the house. Those last to leave he walked out all the way to the bus stop, nearly half a mile away.

To all appearances, Mishi lived a charmed life, and the little house on a gentle slope, with its patio and its orchard, its garden and barbecue pit made up an idyllic scene—a scene from a Gypsy song.

Mishi's pride was his rose garden. To him, the rose was the perfect flower—in fact, perfection itself. He grew other flowers as well—carnations, marigolds, and portulaca, for instance—but he liked them because of their roselike blossoms.

He pruned his rosebushes carefully; he sprayed and fertilized at the recommended intervals. "Growing roses is a matter of discipline," he said. "You have to do what needs to be done and when it needs to be done, and your rosebushes will repay your attention a hundredfold. But, mostly, you have to love them, and they are certain to return your affections."

His rosebushes responded to his expertise. They were unusually vigorous, with good branch structures and with an abundance of blooms year after year.

For as long as a quarter of an hour, Mishi would stand in front of a rosebush, without saying a word and barely moving a muscle, to observe each promising bud, full blossom, and spent petal. "All that's worth loving in the world is summed up in a rose," he liked to say.

After his sixtieth birthday, his knees started giving him trouble, and he tried to tend his roses while sitting in a garden chair or leaning against it. When he no longer had the strength to prune, he had the chair permanently positioned in a spot where he could get the best view. He would sit in the chair and admire the blooms for as long as an hour.

In the city, Mishi lived another life. In the early 1950s, his Armenian benefactor was promoted and transferred back home. When he went to say good-bye to Mishi, he brought along his replacement, a Russian officer who was to serve as Mishi's new mentor—and who quickly became just as fond of Mishi as the Armenian. After the revolution of 1956, when Soviet companies were sold to the Hungarian government as a gesture suggesting increasing independence, Mishi's shop was finally nationalized. But by that time Mishi was considered a trusted, longtime employee—and not as a one-time capitalist owner—and he was retained as the manager until his retirement in the late 1960s.

Mishi's decline began when he stopped going to town at dawn and no longer received his relatives and friends in his office.

The time came when he would not leave his house for months. He bought a television set, but he found the Gypsy musicians and the actresses on the screen "too remote". Family members visited him but did not stay long because his wife was embarrassingly drunk and insulted people.

"It was terrible to look at him," wrote his brother Shumi in a chapter he added to his memoirs. "Our inability to do anything for him hurt. We went to see him often, but I think that our visits did not bring joy to any of us. We always left in despair."

Shumi and other relatives tried to sell the house in Remete and have Mishi and Antzi move to an apartment in Budapest, close to his family. But this time it was Antzi who refused to move.

One by one, his lifelong friends died or became too infirm for the long walk from the bus station to his house, and the rare guest who ventured out to see him had to shout so Mishi could hear. He seemed to have lost interest in politics and the theater. He sat in his favorite chair of carved oak, next to a green tile stove, the same kind that once heated his parents' home in Gyulaj. "Oh I am fine, I am fine," he kept saying, halfheartedly, absentmindedly, allowing himself only two complaints. He said he was always cold, even in the thick sweaters his sisters knitted for him. And he said he could no longer walk without feeling sharp pains in his legs. He could not even walk his guests back to the gate of his house.

For as long as half an afternoon, he would stare wordlessly at the reproduction of a Rembrandt painting which for decades hung above his bed: the portrait of an old soldier with a gleaming, fancy brass helmet but with a tired, haggard face merging into a dark brown background. To cheer him up, somebody would ask Mishi: "Was the art student who copied that Rembrandt for you a blonde or a redhead? Was she sweet or pretty, smart or silly?"

"She was young," was all that Mishi could remember.

He dozed off, and in his dreams he was riding a horse in Gyulaj or driving a car on the endless steppes of Russia.

My mother would remind him of a story. At the age of twenty-one, in Gyulaj, he tried to break in a young horse. But the horse resisted and eventually threw him off.

Villagers found Mishi out in the fields, unconscious, and brought him home gathered up in a bedsheet. The doctor found no bone broken but he diagnosed a severe case of concussion and suggested complete rest in a dark room. After a day, Mishi regained consciousness but not his usual ebullience. He would barely touch his favorite dishes; his best friends could not get him to smile. He didn't even react to the pretty Gypsy girl who was brought in from a neighboring village to entertain him.

The doctor kept advising patience. Weeks passed and

Mishi was listless, depressed, and could not be coaxed out of his room, or even out of bed.

Finally, Shumi, by then the head of the family, had a brilliant idea: one morning he drove the carriage to Nyiregyháza and invited Mishi's friend, the Gypsy violinist Aladár Mantu, to try to cheer Mishi up. Mantu promptly packed his bags and by the evening he was at Mishi's bedside. But Mishi barely recognized him. Then the Gypsy started to play Mishi's favorite songs, very softly, and Mishi sat up in his bed.

Mantu, who was put up in the guest room and was treated like visiting royalty, played his music for most of the following day. By the evening, Mishi got out of bed and started singing. After a few more days of music, Mishi was his old self again.

Showered with presents, Mantu returned to Nyiregyháza, and his fame quickly spread across the county as "a miracle doctor with a violin."

Mishi listened to the story about his youth with the hint of a smile, and then said: "This time, it's too late for a Gypsy."

He reread his favorite novels—by Móric Jókai, the Jókai, who was Mishi's father's favorite writer as well, had had no children. But as a novelist, he gave birth to a cast of thousands: star-crossed lovers who loved but once; women who swore to bring their men to glory or ruin, and did; commoners who defeated kings; villains who, like Shakespeare's Richard III, were determined to be villains. Mishi imagined himself in the company of Jókai's passionate men and women, possessed by dreams or nightmares and carrying out their destinies that were often foretold at birth or determined generations earlier.

There came a time when Mishi hardly spoke and seldom

shaved. His two sisters cried when they saw how little he ate. Ashes from cigarettes forbidden by his doctor flecked his rumpled, threadbare trousers. But he still made his special coffee, even though the doctors urged him to stop drinking it.

His dark hair turned white, his swarthy complexion, ashen. For months, he refused to get a medical checkup. Finally, he consented to see a doctor, a friend from their days from the forced-labor camp, who said that Mishi had arteriosclerosis but that the illness did not explain the precipitous decline of his health. The physician suggested that the strains of Mishi's home life might be responsible for his condition.

Except for his closest relatives, Mishi no longer seemed to appreciate visitors. When his nephew Levente came to show off his newborn daughter, Mishi sat with the baby in his arms and his tears fell on her. "My little girl," he kept saying, "my little girl." He could not stop crying.

"He was born on March 21, 1903, on the first day of spring," his brother Shumi, four years his senior, wrote in his memoirs. "He left us on November 20, 1972, just as the season's first snow started falling. For almost seventy years, we lived near each other in affectionate, unlimited mutual trust. I will always see him as he was in our childhood: sweet, agile, talkative, smart. He joined me in every game, mischief, and adventure. I gave him the nickname Monkey because he copied me, but he did not mind the name. The two of us walked together under the walnut trees of our garden, roamed the meadows and lost our way at the boundaries of our village. We plunged into the forbidden waters of the pond called Brickmaker, and we asked to be picked up by wagons drawn by horses and oxen."

•　　•　　•

At Mishi's funeral there were many women. Some of them were known to the family from his youth; others were strangers. They all brought roses.

One huge bouquet was carried in and placed on the grave by a uniformed delivery man. Golden letters on the black ribbon said: "To my darling Mishi." A cousin counted one hundred red rosebuds.

In 1931, Uncle Mishi is sitting with Betty, vaguely remembered by the family as "one of Mishi's little actresses," and with Aladár Mantu, the Gypsy violinist friend who once "cured" his depression.

My mother Anna and my father Aladár in the late 1930s.

13.

Honeycake, Honeycake

Whither is fled the visionary gleam?
Where is it now, the glory and the dream?
WORDSWORTH, *Intimations of Immortality*
from Recollections of Early Childhood

My mother Anna no longer remembers when she first tasted her cousin Jenny's celebrated honeycake, which for many years was acknowledged as the best in a family that has always loved baking, eating, and judging cakes. In between the two world wars, Jenny's honeycake earned such a compliment not only during the fleeting ecstasies of consumption, but as a result of lengthy comparative analyses in the vanilla-scented languor of many a Sunday afternoon.

Traditionally, a block of honeycake the size of a small apple is eaten to break the fast on Yom Kippur—which is a tribute either to the surge of energy that honey gives, or to the biblical significance of honey as a preferred victual, or possibly both. A honeycake is also served throughout the year as a kind of basic, all-purpose, no-frills cake. As a genre, honeycakes seem to invite comparison and competition, the same way as preserves of, say, apricot and gooseberry do, where the flavor and the texture of the fruits as well as the recipe are gloriously variable. In contrast, the classics of pastry art, such as Hungary's Rigó Jancsi and Indiáner, must always be made exactly the same way, with the slavish precision of a chemist mixing a formula for dynamite.

The honeycake is not without its detractors; it has even been called a poor relative to "true" pastry. Historians trace its origins to the Ottoman empire—where pashas and peasants alike craved dough laced with honey, and sweeter was synonymous with better—and, further back in time, to pharaonic Egypt, which worshipped honey. Some commentators on Hungarian cuisine contend that honeycakes constitute a class below such delicately balanced chocolate-and-walnut cakes as Diós Torta or Dobos, which owe their inspiration to Vienna and Paris.

Compared to such symphonies of butter and flour and sugar, chocolate and nuts and fruit preserves, the honeycake stands out as having a melody that is at the same time primitive and sophisticated, elemental and mysterious—much like a choice folk tune. And just as a swig of plum brandy leaves on the palate the aftertaste of fresh plums, honey's intriguing flavor—so different from the simple sweetness of sugar—lingers in the mouth.

Born in the 1870s, Cousin Jenny was a homebody who lived in a fine house on a quiet, elm-lined street in the provincial town of Debrecen. Her father, Lajos—named after Lajos Kossuth, the leader of Hungary's 1848 revolution—was the eldest of Samuel Schwarcz's eight children and also the wealthiest because, following Jewish law, Lajos had received one half of his father's wealth. As one of his five children, Jenny inherited a goodly portion, and, moreover, she married a wealthy man who died suddenly when she was still in her twenties. To her relatives, Jenny was a bit of a mystery: a smart, elegant, well-educated widow who never remarried. She had good looks and refined manners, and she lived with her one child, Lily, who was in her twenties in the 1930s, and looked and acted just like Jenny.

Except to visit relatives, Jenny rarely left her home, and Lily, who worked in an office near the house, did not like to go out. Lily turned down invitations by the most handsome men in town and would not give a reason. Like other women on their rung of the social ladder—and they qualified as haute bourgeoisie—they received visitors once a week: from five o'clock to eight every Sunday except during the heat of August, and an hour earlier during winter. This Hungarian equivalent of the English tea centered around several varieties of freshly baked pastry, the product of one's household, served on silver platters and eaten off dainty plates of fine china, with a silver dessert fork. At times, bite-size squares and triangles of "English-style tea sandwiches" were also served. But a far more popular attraction was the *pogácsa*, a salty biscuit flavored with cumin seeds or grated cabbage or cheese, which has a taste suggesting the English scone, even though its lineage is Asian, going back to the Turkish *bogaca* made by nomads in the ashes of the fires built in the evening to keep the people warm and their food ready for eating in the morning.

On a low table covered with a starched white tablecloth edged with lace, Jenny presented freshly roasted coffee in a large pot of delicate china—white with gold trim and red rosebuds hovering over its belly—and surrounded by matching cups and saucers. The set contained one pitcher for hot milk, and a larger and more elaborate one for whipped cream, which the white-uniformed maid whipped, under Jenny's watchful eyes, only minutes before the guests started arriving. (The maid prepared another batch an hour later, in response to a pre-arranged signal from Jenny.) For the children, who were seated together in a corner away from the Persian carpets, there was plenty of steaming hot chocolate, which burned the lips of the over-eager, but which had to be boiling hot for an educational reason. "You must wait until it cools off," someone not necessarily one's mother would caution. "You must learn to be patient." Gobs of whipped cream were plopped on top of the hot chocolate, accompanied by advice that no child needed: "Fresh cream is good for you."

On any given Sunday, as many as twenty relatives mingled with a handful of close friends. Women and older people were seated, and men, particularly young men, stood. Most people dropped in—"for only a few minutes, really, just to say hello." Everyone in the family kissed everyone else on both cheeks, and a young man, such as my uncle Mishi—freshly shaven and proud of his aftershave lotion, and wearing his best suit newly pressed—honored each of his older female relatives with an additional kiss on the hand. My aunt Mara arrived out of breath, her one silk dress rustling. She promptly announced "I've got to run; I have things to do," and then sat down and gave a thirty-minute account of a neighbor who grew an unbelievably beautiful new variety of dahlia. "You look wonderful, Mara," an aunt said in response. "When are you getting married?"

Most people stayed for two or three hours, and a visit of less than one hour would have been considered rude. Not showing up had its risks: relatives and friends not present provided inevitable targets for investigation. For instance, a cousin who had just had a red dress made—"perhaps a bit too red" was the cautious opening salvo—prompted the comment that, "She already has too many dresses, why did she need a red one?" Someone of a conservative bent said that she had heard the dress described as "daring." Then my mother Anna, who classified herself a "progressive person in favor of moving in step with the times," cleverly foiled the criticism by testifying that the dress was "a bit old-fashioned, actually, if you look at it from up close."

A sensitive subject, discussed in hushed tones by three cousins huddled in a corner, was the reason a certain aunt was no longer on speaking terms with another aunt. (Both of them were absent, clearly to avoid a possible confrontation.) After all the details of which aunt hurt the other's feelings first were debated, and historical antecedents established, the final assessment was neutral. Even where justified, the adoption of a partisan position would not have been appropriate—and certainly not at the forum of Cousin Jenny's Sunday coffee, which no discordant note was allowed to disrupt. The right thing to do was to express hope for a reconciliation, and preferably before the next family wedding or birth.

My mother gave an enthusiastic report on her latest visit to her mother's older brother in Ungvár, "who looked twenty years younger than his age and whose granddaughter is turning into one of the most sought-after young girls in town." She added that she was saving money to travel to see cousins in Huszt. Both towns were within an eighty-mile radius, but across the border in politically hostile Czechoslovakia, which provoked Zoltán, a cousin fifteen years her senior, to ask, "If you could please explain, no offense meant, why you are always itching to be travelling, even abroad." "I like to be on the go," was my mother's cheerful reply, and another older cousin came to her defense by recalling how much her father used to like to travel. The legacy of a family trait thus clarified, Zoltán promptly beat a retreat by declaring how much he "loved that dear, dear man no longer with us."

The fortunes of Debrecen's own soccer team Bocskay— usually in decline—was an unwelcome subject, not only because the town went into churlish mourning after each defeat, but also because athletes with their crude display of physical prowess were not considered as deserving mention in polite society. Yet the young generation's strange new interests included soccer, and Bocskay claimed the loyalty of several family members. Someone tolerant, such as my grandmother Róza, asked her son Anti, known to attend every Bocskay game in town, "But why can't our boys score a goal?" The question, expressed with a great deal of sympathy for the team, prompted a long explanation. But she was the only one to listen. And once more Róza would promise her son to go with him to see her first soccer game one day soon.

Politics, a matter of intense interest mostly to the men, was another topic of conversation of borderline propriety. Only a relative visiting from a smaller town or village anxious to learn about the outside world, or a journalist friend in a rumpled suit and with a stained tie, would mention a name such as Adolf Hitler's. A contemptuous look or a remark "madmen who are not worth talking about" would bring any discussion to a quick end.

The platters were replenished with pastry, and a fresh pot of coffee was brought in. "I must go," someone said. "Please stay," Jenny replied, and everyone did.

As the volume of conversation kept rising, the hands of the grandfather clock seemed to move most reluctantly, and the shadows of the afternoon deepened into twilight at a gentle pace. Women kept peering through the lace-curtained windows to see whether it might not be getting too late. They liked to be home before dark, and said so a few times, even though the streets they lived on were well lit and safe, and their homes were no farther than a fifteen-minute walk. Whenever they decided to leave—and Jenny talked them into staying a bit longer even after they put on their coats and were standing in the vestibule—they could be certain of an offer from a gallant male relative, sometimes twenty years older, sometimes twenty years younger and, on occasion, of about the same age, to walk them home, arm in arm. Yet no one, not even the most gossipy neighbors, would suggest that there might be anything but family feeling to the public intimacy they witnessed.

Though Cousin Jenny was a versatile baker who liked to try many different recipes, she had one item she served nearly every Sunday: her honeycake. Cut with a sharp knife into precise diamonds, it had a soft, creamy filling which nobody could identify for certain but which was a perfect complement to the layer of preserves, homemade of course. Jenny's favorites were raspberry and plum. To her, raspberries represented innocence, and plum, abundance, and these were two qualities she admired.

Members of the family who travelled widely and sampled the honeycakes of other households and other lands thought that Jenny's honeycake was the softest, the creamiest, and the most delicate honeycake they had ever tasted. They thought it was unquestionably superior to the spicy, heavy, and often dry honeycakes of Romania, made with cloves and cardamom, and topped with almond slivers—which tasted better with a splash of plum brandy or wine—as well as to the gooey concoctions of Yugoslavia, Greece, and Turkey dripping with honey and crammed with walnuts or filberts, or both. Jenny's honeycake was on another level, the connoisseurs decided, it was in a class of its own.

When she was complimented, Jenny said "thank you" in a way some family members thought was a bit curt—almost dismissive, in fact—and then she went on discussing the concerts she had been to or the books she had been reading.

My mother, some thirty years younger than Jenny and a rival when it came to baking, was fascinated by Jenny's aplomb. And she was most curious about Jenny's honeycake.

Jenny had her own way of telling a recipe—or, rather, of not telling it. She was too well mannered to refuse to answer a direct question on what she put in the cake. So she would list the obvious ingredients—honey, flour, and preserves—and then she made the process of baking sound easy, much too easy. But if someone asked her about quantities and proportions, she would respond with a discourse on the meaninglessness of numbers. Or, if she was in a different mood, she would say that some numbers were unlucky for her—for instance five—while other numbers, like three and seven, represented the proportions of the universe and were thus truly mystical and profoundly significant.

If my mother or some other relative somehow succeeded in returning to the subject of the recipe for her honeycake, Jenny would sigh and say how puzzling it was to her that people always seemed to be interested in her baking, even though, to tell the truth, baking interested her very little, and those who understood her well knew that. And in a second, she was talking about rereading *Madame Bovary* and how she found Flaubert at times cruel to his heroine, who was not at all as shallow and flighty as she was described, but, instead, a helpless victim of her men—one man, mostly: her husband.

Someone prosaic would counter that Madame Bovary was the creature of a writer's imagination and that it was pointless to talk about her as a person who lived and who therefore invited our sympathy.

Jenny would give the person a look that would wither a

My mother Anna on Debrecen's Main Street,
now called the Street of the Red Army.

rosebud. That would be the end of her giving mood. Nor would she succumb to my mother's blandishments to give away any part of the recipe for the honeycake.

"Jenny liked secrets," says my mother, who also likes secrets but prefers to be in on them. "Not giving something away made Jenny feel more mysterious and therefore more appreciated."

Like her brothers and sisters and most of her cousins, Jenny also was deported to Auschwitz, where she was killed. Her daughter, Lily had committed suicide a few years earlier in 1941. No one knows the reason, though a love affair with a married man in her office was suspected at the time. They both took their secrets with them.

But my mother could not forget the taste of Jenny's honeycake. Even while Jenny was alive, my mother collected hints and stray bits of information on what might have gone into it, and she tested out her suspicions. She produced many slabs of hard, often inedible cakes before she came up with a satisfactory formula.

The following recipe is a result of the experiments, which she conducted, on and off, for close to twenty years:

In a small pan, put one fourth of a stick—or one ounce—of unsalted butter, one cup of sugar, four tablespoons of milk, and three tablespoons of honey. (Any kind of honey will do, but the dark honey of wildflowers imparts a robust, gritty taste to the cake, and the blonde honey of acacia blossoms or lavender yields the most delicate scents.) Mix it, stir it. Warm it over low flame and let cool.

Then take five cups of all-purpose flour, and sift it with

one tablespoon of baking soda. Put the mixture on a flat surface, make a well and break an egg over it. Mix it all up with your hands. Add to it the contents of the small pan, make a dough, knead it to uniform consistency. Divide it into four parts and shape them into balls. Cover them and let rest for one hour.

Using a rolling pin, roll flat each ball large enough for a cookie sheet 10 by 15 inches. (Don't forget to butter the cookie sheets before placing the dough on them.) Bake the dough in a preheated 375 degree oven until the surface has a golden brown color. Be careful, the dough burns quickly. Remove the cake from the oven.

Let all sheets stand overnight, at room temperature.

Before going to bed that evening, prepare the filling:

Cook in a pan four tablespoons of cream of wheat—nobody, but nobody, will guess that the filling is cream of wheat—in a pint of milk with a drop of vanilla extract. Stir while it cooks.

Let it cool to room temperature.

Add to the cream of wheat two sticks of unsalted butter —eight ounces—with one and one fourth cup of sugar and one egg, then beat it fluffy with a beater.

Put the filling in the refrigerator and go to bed.

Next morning or evening, put half of the filling on the first cookie sheet of prebaked dough. (The dough will be hard, but don't worry, it is supposed to be hard.) Put the second sheet on top of the first and spread on your favorite preserves—but thinly. (The preserves should not be too sweet. Apricot and sour cherry are ideal because of their tartness.) Then put the third sheet on top with the second half of the filling, and, finally, the last sheet on top. Concerned with the appearance of the cake, my mother recommends that the worst-looking sheet should be at the bottom—hiding—and that the nicest-looking sheet be on the top.

Let it stand for at least six hours. Not a minute less.

The surprise is that the cake softens by itself. My mother is not sure if that is because the honey soaks up moisture or because the honey interacts with the cream of wheat. Or perhaps both.

The cake should be cut with a sharp knife into small squares, which is what my mother likes, or into diamonds, which is what Jenny preferred.

The virtue this cake requires from the baker is patience. One must let the dough and the filling rest at all stages.

From time to time, pedants in the family have contended that this particular honeycake belongs in the genre of the torte because its consistency is torte-like and its dominant taste is creamy—which is an attribute of tortes and not of honeycakes. However, my mother and her supporters argue, it is unquestionably the honey that imparts the cake's critical flavor, which lingers in the mouth for minutes after the last morsels are consumed.

My mother regards the honeycake as the best number in her considerable repertoire—the high C of her art. It is also her statement on the human condition: at its best, life is light and sweet, and layered with mystery.

But she is the first one to say that her honeycake is not as good as the one Cousin Jenny last baked nearly half a century ago. Relatives who remember disagree, and give my mother top marks. Well, yes, she says, maybe it comes close, but it is not the same. No.

Having won accolades from family and friends on two continents, my mother no longer conducts experiments to produce an even more faithful reconstruction of Jenny's masterpiece. The recipe described above is her final version.

14.

The Last Landowner
Returns Home

The wild-dove hath her nest, the fox his cave,
Mankind their country—Israel but the grave.
Byron, *Hebrew Melodies*

The land my ancestors contracted to lease in Szabolcs
County—now the northeastern bulge of the Hungarian
republic—at least as far back as the seventeenth century, but probably several centuries earlier, was wandering,
windblown sand, not much better suited for raising crops than
sand dunes on a beach. The noblemen who had been rewarded
by kings for bravery, or some other feat of loyalty, with plots
of land and serfs to work them owned everything as far as
the eye could see on the flat terrain, and beyond. But they
could not turn much of a profit and were happy to find somebody foolish enough to risk money and effort on such an
unpromising tract of land.

The central mystery of my family history is why and how
my ancestors—who must have included peddlers and merchants who travelled from village to village, from county to
county, earning a modest living—decided to settle down in
a little-known nook of Szabolcs County, turned to agriculture,
acquired an abiding love of the land, learned superior farming
techniques, and eventually bought titles to a sizeable acreage.
How did they become so passionately attached to this remote
patch of earth?

Shumi as the young master at age twelve.

Other Jews were always on the move. The highway was their homeland, even though, as the saying went, there were only three professions to practice on the road: to rob, to beg, and to trade. Jews did only the last two and feared those engaged in the first. They bought sacks of wheat in the Great Plain, barrels of wine in the Tokay region, and crates of cups and plates of tin and silver in Transylvania, and carted them to Bohemia and Silesia to the north, and to the Balkans to the south. The poorest Jews walked from village to village for charity, and the most influential were those who lent money or managed the treasuries of the powerful in the realms of the Turkish sultan, the Habsburg emperor, the Transylvanian prince.

Yet from generation to generation, my ancestors chose to stay put and till the soil in the vicinity of Derzs, a tiny village at the end of a road seldom travelled, far from the main highways. They did not wish to be known in the county; they did not flaunt their successes. What to others must have been the far end of the world was to my family a safe haven, if not a Garden of Eden.

Unlike other Jews, my forebears strongly opposed marriages between cousins, even second and third cousins. When the men married, they imported brides from neighboring counties, sometimes even farther. But they tried to keep daughters nearby and usually found them husbands in Szabolcs County.

From the nineteenth or perhaps the late eighteenth century on, my ancestors planted locust trees, a fast-growing new import from the colony of Virginia in the New World, to block the remorseless wind from the Carpathian mountains which blew away the topsoil and exposed the roots of plants. They also gathered all the dead foliage and all the manure they could find and plowed them under, year after year. "Nothing should go to waste," was the family motto, and if the legend is accurate, they had a compost pile many decades if not a century before it was invented early in this century by a British agronomist in India.

By the last decades of the nineteenth century, their persistence had paid off. They harvested bumper crops of wheat and potatoes; they had fine orchards of apple, pear, and above all, apricots, as well as fields of tobacco and vegetables. When my great-grandfather Samuel Schwarcz died in 1895, he had much land to distribute among his eight children, and some of them, like my grandfather Karl, kept buying more land.

However, the very first plot of land my ancestors purchased—several centuries before the mid–1800s when Jews could first legally own land in Hungary—was for a cemetery of their own. This half-acre was off a winding back road, about a mile from the family home in Derzs. Two generations ago, the cemetery was still at least half a mile from the last house in the village; today, the village is expanding in its direction, and a house now stands next to it. Though the cemetery is on a slight rise, centuries ago it was bounded by a ditch for additional protection from floodwaters that sometimes cover large parts of the insistently flat terrain.

While Jewish tradition calls for a funeral within forty-eight hours after death, and Christian villagers strongly object to having a corpse carried across a village boundary for fear of unleashing evil spirits, even family members who sought their fortune elsewhere in Szabolcs County were often brought to be laid to rest in the Derzs cemetery, in accordance with their last wishes. As required by their Jewish faith, they were buried in plain, unplaned pine coffins, constructed without nails, which fell apart in a decade or so along with the corpse, becoming part of the soil and enriching it. As the Bible says: "For dust you are, and to dust you shall return."

My mother, Anna, remembers that at least once a year, usually on a fine sunny day in fall, between the New Year and the Day of Atonement, her father used to take a cartload of his children, as well as whatever nephews and nieces happened to be around, to visit the family cemetery. He taught them the custom of putting a pebble on a grave—a simple little gesture which says to the person buried there: "I have been here, I have thought of you."

He pointed to the graves of his parents Samuel and Taube, and told stories about his courage and her wisdom. He used to say that Samuel remained an enterprising young man all his life and that even white-bearded rabbis listened when Taube spoke. The idea behind the outing seemed to be that children should not be afraid of death and the dead, but should think of their departed ancestors as parts of themselves and accept the end of life the way they accept birth. He cited the holy books which describe a child as born with fists clenched, as if to say that "the whole world is mine," and when the person dies, the hands are outstretched and empty, as if to say, "I have inherited nothing from this world."

"My father brought us to the cemetery to make sure that we learned that it was ours and that we belonged there," my mother wrote in her memoirs, "and that we won't forget those already resting there." He pointed with his walking stick to the space where he intended to be buried—much the same way that he would point to a plot of land he hoped to buy one day or to one he owned already and planned to turn into an orchard. He said he hoped his children would visit his grave, and that when the time came, they too would find their final home there.

Having visited the cemetery several times in the 1970s and '80s, my mother has the satisfaction of having complied with one part of her father's wish. But she is apologetic that as a resident of Budapest, it is too complicated for her to arrange to be buried there.

Another puzzling question in our family history is how the Schwarcz estate of thousands of acres, acquired little by little over so many years, came to be lost. After all, each of my grandfather's brothers married well, and their wives' dowries helped purchase more land. Each of the brothers set up his own estate, and each stayed in Szabolcs County, within half a day's carriage ride from one another. But one by one they all went bankrupt in this century, even before Adolf Hitler's shadow fell across Hungary.

Like the Roman destruction of the Temple in Jerusalem— for which the Talmud offers pages upon pages of detailed and seemingly conflicting explanations—the fall of the Schwarcz fortune has prompted several analyses. The one that seems the most likely is that the seven brothers bought more land than they could manage or pay for, and that they invested too much money in equipment, much of which was stolen during the two revolutions that followed the First World War and then during the Romanian occupation. Yet another theory is that the seven brothers were tied to one another in complicated financial arrangements, most of them without the benefit of contracts or anything committed to writing, and that one bankruptcy precipitated another.

When one asks for a single reason that brought about the fall, villagers and the oldest members of my family have the same answer: "The war," by which they mean the First World War, the storm which also blew away Habsburgs, Hohenzollerns, and Romanoffs, and shattered the European order of a thousand years.

The last Schwarcz landowner in Gyulaj was my grandfather's eldest son: Samuel according to his birth certificate, but known to everyone by his childhood nickname, Shumi. He was twenty-one at the time he took over the estate, fresh from the Italian front where he had been a candidate officer in the Habsburg emperor's defeated army. He had a high school diploma, but no profession or trade, and his interests were characteristic of the landed gentry.

My mother remembers how one bright summer morning her two big brothers, Shumi and Mishi, took off on the best carriage of the household, pulled by the two nicest-looking horses from the stable, to "live it up a little." They visited Nyiregyháza, where they went to see the operetta *The Csardas Queen* and sent a bouquet of roses the size of a cartwheel to the prima donna along with a brief note that asked her "to accept the gift of two young hearts" and requested "the favor of a meeting." With sea green eyes, a pearly complexion, and a crown of lustrous dark hair, the prima donna reigned on and off stage. (A few years later, she quit the theater after her marriage to an old, wealthy count, whose forebears had distinguished themselves fighting the Ottoman Turks and plotting against the Habsburgs. Their son was a classmate of mine, and in the early 1950s, on the street in front of our school, Shumi recognized her, by then a gray-haired widow in a tired raincoat and with a face to match. Shumi introduced himself as an unreconstructed admirer, bowed from the waist and delivered one of the great hand kisses of history.)

But that summer night of long ago, she was inaccessible, and Shumi and Mishi consoled themselves by inviting two chorus girls who had never before visited Szabolcs County to a champagne dinner. Around midnight, they all went for a long ride to see the countryside in its leafy glory, with a Gypsy violinist in the back of the carriage and the moon as their silent partner.

"When the boys finally returned home a few days later," my mother recalls, in a tone blending pride with exasperation, "they were riding a crude peasant cart, pulled by two strange, spavined nags." Having run out of cash, Shumi and Mishi pawned their fine carriage and sold their horses, handed out generous tips, and then made their way home with whatever transport they could buy from the money left over.

In Gyulaj, he could not stop the slide to disaster, and he could never forgive himself for that failure. As explanations—though not as excuses—he suggested his youthful inexperience with people, his lamentable lack of agricultural know-how, and his hot temper that prevented his coming to terms with his weak, indecisive uncle Albert who was egged on by his strong-willed and malicious wife. Shumi also found the climate of the post-war years harsh and unpredictable, laden with deception and distrust, and markedly different from the era of faith and hope in which his father and grandfather had lived and prospered. Nevertheless, for the rest of his life Shumi blamed himself for because the loss of the family inheritance took place while he was in charge.

Nor was he a satisfactory eldest son to his father, and here was another failure for which he sought to make amends in his old age. Looking back on his life in the 1960s, it occurred to him that one fault might well have been what his father

251

called "godlessness." His father had begged him not to forget his prayers and to keep the Sabbath. His last letter to him had ended with a warning: "Remember, there is a God!"

"But I couldn't believe, and I still can't," Shumi explained decades later, "and I couldn't and wouldn't pretend." He suggested that he might have sealed his fate when he stopped observing the laws of Moses at age seventeen, after he was sent off to a military academy to be trained as an army officer.

In his memoirs, Shumi recalled a visit to Rabbi Yissachar Dov of Belz, the same wise man who nearly a quarter of a century earlier had advised his father to look for "another Rachel Kaufmann" to marry. After Shumi's father had indeed found the second Rachel Kaufmann, he became a devoted follower of the Rabbi of Belz, visiting him at least once a year and asking for his advice on important decisions. Every fall, after the High Holy Days, carts loaded with sacks of the finest wheat flour, the fattest geese, and the largest goose liver were sent from his house in Gyulaj to the rabbi in Galitzia, nearly three hundred miles to the northeast and now part of the Soviet Union.

For a long time, the Rabbi of Belz had been asking to see Shumi, but his father kept postponing a visit even though he had promised it more than once. "The postponement was an embarrassment for my father," Shumi wrote. "It was because he was ashamed of the fact that I did not speak Yiddish."

Because of the Great War raging in and around Belz, an ancient walled town then belonging to the Austro-Hungarian monarchy but claimed by Poland and Russia as well, the rabbi fled with hundreds of his congregants across the Carpathian mountains and set up temporary headquarters in a Hungarian village a few hours' carriage ride from Gyulaj. His household was called a court, and it was a court in the traditional sense of the word: administrators kept au courant with faithful subjects and their contributions; courtiers sized up visitors and arranged for the favor of seeing the king immediately or later, for a short or a long period of time. On any given day, scores of petitioners asked to see the Rabbi of Belz, who had a reputation of being saintly yet practical— equally knowledgeable about the mysteries of the Talmud, the complexities of business, and the hearts of men and women. He also invited people for holy days, which were celebrated in opulent style, and his expositions of biblical passages set people's souls on fire.

On one occasion when Shumi was on home leave from the officers' academy, his father decided finally to wait no longer, and he took his eldest son to meet with the rabbi. On the way, the father was uncharacteristically tense and worried, and he instructed his son to speak as little as possible in front of the rabbi.

They were ceremoniously received by the rabbi's chief chamberlain, whom Shumi described as "a black-bearded, intelligent diplomat. He treated us most respectfully and invited us to his house, where we had tea with an unforgettable taste, laced with choice Tokay wine, and we were offered a two-pound chunk of goose liver. Then he dispatched a note to the rabbi that we were there. Sending away his followers who surrounded him, the rabbi let us know that he was ready to receive us right away."

Shumi wrote that when they were admitted to the rabbi's presence, he was "instantly enchanted by the patriarch," whose eyes reflected "intelligence and understanding." The dignified bearing and the immaculate black garb made a strong impression on Shumi. Befitting his status as a cadet in uniform, he stood at attention, saluted, and clicked his heels—and then kissed the rabbi's hand.

"He put his hands over my head, blessed me, and expressed his joy over meeting me," Shumi wrote. "Then he said, in pure, classical German, caressing my head: 'I see that you are well dressed, that things are going well for you, that you are not suffering on the front. But I would like to know whether you keep kosher.'

"This was a terrible question. My father was looking at me, and I felt I had to lie.

" 'I do,' I said.

" 'I am glad to hear that,' the rabbi said. 'But remember: things will always go well for you as long as you observe the laws of our faith.'

"On the way home—and it was a long journey—my father did not say a word to me. I too kept quiet and was ashamed of myself."

In 1927, Shumi, as head of the family, moved his mother and his six brothers and sisters to Debrecen, then a city with a population of a little over one hundred thousand. An uncle lent money to rent a small house and to start a new life. The land so lovingly tended by generations was lost forever, becoming an aching memory not dulled by time. For years to come, Shumi dreamt that he still lived in Gyulaj, which he and his brothers and sisters never ceased to refer to as "home."

No longer belonging to the privileged class of landed gentry and out of place in a town of merchants and wealthy peasants, Shumi found a job with a wine distributor and worked in a dim, dank cellar. He studied in the evenings and soon qual-

Clockwise, from the top: Uncle Shumi at age thirteen; his
army ID from the First World War; in 1945; in 1981.

ified as a bookkeeper. In the years to come, he found a measure of satisfaction in acquiring the skills of maintaining good order in ledgers and in balancing books.

Exile had a sobering effect on him. Unlike his brother Mishi, he did not spend his time in coffeehouses and around theaters, but worked long hours instead. Determined to build a modest, middle-class life, Shumi tried hard to forget that he had once been a member of the most prominent family in a village.

He took care of his mother, as he had promised to his father, spending at least half an hour with her every day, even after his marriage. His wife, Agnes, was a traditional Jewish woman, pious and hardworking. She first gave birth to a sickly son, who was named after Shumi's father but who died after a few days. Then she bore a healthy, red-headed daughter, named Kati after someone in Agnes' family. Kati was freckle-faced, talkative, and cheerful—a typical Schwarcz.

Pinching pennies, Shumi and Agnes managed to buy on the outskirts of the city, a small house with a big yard. Shumi planted and pruned fruit trees and rosebushes, and Agnes saved money by tending a vegetable garden. They both worked hard to bring back to life the neglected fruit trees they had found on the property and which included a young, promising walnut tree.

At the beginning of the Second World War Shumi was drafted, and his forced-labor battalion was dispatched to dig ditches and build tank traps to stop the Red Army. Toward the end of the war, he escaped and hid in a cellar belonging to a scion of one of Debrecen's leading families. "Before the war, that man, a patrician, would not condescend to say 'good day' to me," Shumi said later. As the thunder of the Russian artillery became louder and more insistent, the patrician decided that Shumi was his close friend. He also asked Shumi to open the cellar door when the Russians entered the courtyard and banged on the doors. "You are a relative of Stalin," the patrician said, half in jest. It was his way of saying that as someone who was persecuted under the pro-Nazi regime, Shumi could expect better treatment from the communists.

Shumi did not think of himself as a relative of Stalin, but when the Russians did occupy Debrecen, his friends from the forced-labor battalion suggested he take part in the denazification program promoted by the Red Army and they talked Shumi into joining the new "democratic" police force. Though he accepted the rank of a captain, Shumi refused to wear a uniform. Some of his friends joined the Communist Party, because it seemed to them that the Russian communists were the only true enemies of the German and Hungarian Nazis, and a few of his friends were determined to avenge the murder of their families.

Shumi criticized the new regime's reliance on informants in tracking down Hungarian Nazis and his new colleagues' readiness to make snap judgments about people who might not have been guilty. "We should go after the criminals who killed people," he argued, "but we should not seek indiscriminate revenge." A phrase he then used for the first time became his credo later: "We must not become like the Nazis."

When a close friend of his from the forced-labor battalion was named a colonel in the newly formed secret police, which was modelled after the Soviets', and pleaded with Shumi to join and accept "a leading role in purging the country," Shumi's response was to quit the police. Then, and for years to come, he said he saw little difference between Stalin and Hitler. He warned his friends that joining the communists was "an irreparable, tragic mistake" that they and their children and their children's children would regret. He was convinced that, because communism was an alien system and a dictatorship, Hungarians would sooner or later reject it with an anger commensurate with the repression practiced by the communists.

In early 1945, Shumi moved to Budapest, where most of the family decided to live. It was in my parents' apartment on a Buda hillside that he and the rest of the family heard the testimony confirming what Shumi and others had suspected for a long time: his wife and their daughter, his mother, and his older sister had been killed in Auschwitz.

"There is no meaning to my life," Shumi declared. "There is no reason for me to go on." He acknowledged he was contemplating suicide.

The family's response was to invite him for long strolls and to have the relatives he was most fond of tell him about their plans to start anew. The children were instructed to accompany him on errands and to ask him for help with homework. "Keep him walking and keep him talking," my mother urged me, though perhaps the order had originated with Aunt Mara speaking to her son, Levente.

Uncle Shumi was good company. Ignoring the sight of houses pockmarked with bullet holes or crumpled by bombs in the fighting that had ended only a few months earlier, he talked about a deeper past. Climbing Rózsadomb—which means the Hill of Roses—he suggested a visit to the tomb of Gül Baba, the seventeenth century Turkish pasha whose name means Father of Roses and who had grown the finest roses in the sultan's realm. Nothing was left of the pasha's pleasure garden overlooking the Danube, but Shumi could conjure up the colors and the fragrances. He liked to wander through the ruined fortress of Várhegy, which means Castle Hill, where Hungary's kings had ruled for centuries and where waves of invaders for two millennia had fought some of their fiercest battles. He pointed to blocked entrances in the stone walls. "This hill is like an ant hill," he said, "full of tunnels." He wanted to sneak inside and explore, and was sheepish when a policeman appeared and warned him that entry was both against the law and common sense because corpses of soldiers from the most recent war were still moldering in the passageways.

The limestone of the Buda hills is surprisingly soft, and its and the surface, the color of the moon, invites initials and messages. Shumi pointed to rocks jutting out of a steep slope and suggested we look for inscriptions in Hungarian, Russian, or German, in Turkish or Latin. We found names and many a heart pierced with an arrow—and a countless number of scorings that must have been the work of human hands but whose meanings were blurred by wind and rain.

Shumi cut himself a stick with a penknife he always carried with him, and now and then he poked the soil. He shook his head in disapproval when encountering clay, which he thought was an unsatisfactory compromise between soil and stone. He called clay "stubborn" and "greedy." He meant that clay absorbed rain and would not let it drain, even if that led to an overdose of water choking the roots of plants. He praised "the wisdom of sand" in letting water pass through and mixing well with whatever improvements—manure, straw, or compost—a good steward of the land might add.

Going home, we sometimes waited for a tram. Rounding a corner, the wheels squeaked and sounded like crows driven off a carcass, and the spiderlike connectors linking the carriage to the overhead electric lines kept showering sparks that smelled of sulfur. "Let's walk to the next station," Shumi suggested, or he argued for a shortcut across the hill. He always preferred to walk.

His pace was brisk, and he hurried as if he had promised to be somewhere by a certain time. He did not like to take the same route twice. He walked the way a lawyer cross-examines: in a forceful search for a useful truth.

In the first few years after the war, the family had many meetings with long agendas. But the basic question was always the same: what to do in a world not to our liking.

Shortly after the communists seized power in 1948 and "nationalized" trade, industry, and even small firms, Shumi found a modest job as a bookkeeper with the state company that bred horses. It took him three hours by train to go back and forth between his home in Budapest and the provincial town where he worked, for less pay than he would have earned in a similar job in Budapest. But, strangely enough, he did not try to change jobs.

He married again—but he did not want another child.

For close to twenty years after the Second World War, Uncle Shumi rarely spoke of his native village of Gyulaj. Talking to the children in the family, he told stories about his father and other ancestors, but the focus was on their character, not the place whence they came or the land they had cultivated. In a lighthearted way, he merely said it was better to have lost the family estate "honorably"—as a result of the war and his ineptness—than to have it expropriated by the communists.

Though he never put on any airs as head of the family, he felt the responsibility of his position. In his elaborate, nineteenth century style, he wrote letters to far-flung relatives and kept in touch with everyone. He discovered third and fourth cousins the family had not heard from for decades. He kept track of birthdays, and he was especially conscientious in congratulating parents on the birth of a child. After his retirement in the late 1960s, he wrote his family history, some one hundred pages, single-spaced and without margins.

The wall opposite his desk was covered with photographs of the children in the family. His nephews and nieces and more distant cousins growing up in Israel and North America were crowded into the same frames with the few who remained in Hungary. Among the glossy color photographs was a yellowing black-and-white one of his daughter Kati, the last one taken before she was killed in Auschwitz at age five.

When my daughter was born in 1979, in Washington, D.C., we gave her the name Malka Haya. In his congratulatory letter, Shumi expressed his joy at having a new grandniece. Then he mentioned in one matter-of-fact sentence, almost parenthetically, what I had not known: his daughter Kati's Hebrew name was Haya Malka. A rationalist, Shumi did not make anything of the coincidence.

In the mid-1960s he surprised everyone by announcing his plan to be buried in the family cemetery in Derzs, which he had visited only once since the move to Debrecen in 1927.

But the problems seemed insurmountable.

No one had been buried there since the family left the village, and Hungarian law was as clear as it was practical: a cemetery unused for thirty years is considered abandoned, and if no one is buried in a village cemetery for more than a generation, the land should be returned to normal, that is to say, agricultural, use.

Shumi's second wife, Ily, was horrified by the idea of her husband wanting to be buried in such a remote, hard-to-reach place. Her first husband had died somewhere in Russia as a member of a forced-labor battalion and was buried no one knows where. Should she be deprived of the chance to visit her second husband's grave as well? She knew, she said, that she was only "a substitute wife" because Shumi's "real wife" was the first one, Agnes, who had died because she would not leave her daughter who was dispatched to the gas chamber. "There is not a day that Shumi does not remember them," Ily said. But as Shumi's wife since 1950, did she not have the right to bury her husband in Budapest, where she could visit his grave regularly?

Uncle Shumi refused to bow to reality.

Every year or two he visited the village, undeterred by the fact that the journey from Budapest took a day, with a train and two buses. On his first visit, he was accompanied by a relative, and to get to the graves, they had to push through a dense thicket of locust trees that had sprouted from scattered seeds. They were talking when they noticed a group of children, looking at them from the road, a distance of some one hundred yards. "There are ghosts in the cemetery," one child shouted to the others. "The dead Jews have come back," cried another, and they ran home to tell their parents.

Two world wars, occupations by foreign armies, and indigenous revolutions had worked changes in the local population, which had doubled to eight hundred in a generation, but Shumi did find a few old villagers who remembered him and who had only kind words for the Schwarcz family. He also made friends with the school teacher and the priest of the Greek Catholic church, both newcomers to the village. From Budapest he wrote to the school children who were surprised to learn that some Jews were still alive in the world. He visited the school and attended classes for the Greek Catholic children in the parish. It did not take long for the children to start appreciating the kind old gentleman who was always delighted to tell stories about life in the village long, long ago.

From the mid-1970s on, whenever he visited the village Uncle Shumi was asked by the children to tell a family story, such as the one about his ancestor Itzig Schwarcz. Overcome by grief that he had to bury his only son, Lazar, Itzig went to the cemetery several times a week to pray at the grave. He neglected his family, his work.

Finally, his wife approached the rabbi for advice. The rabbi suggested that the family stage the funeral again, with everyone participating who had been there the first time, and that he, the rabbi, would deliver the same eulogy.

The idea sounded strange, but the family agreed because a rabbi's advice is a rabbi's advice.

But when the rabbi completed the ceremony, there was a last act which was different: he and an assistant turned over the tombstone so the inscription faced the ground and could no longer be read.

And indeed, the father found peace after the second funeral.

Every year, Shumi's links with the village grew stronger. He persuaded relatives visiting from Israel and Canada to pay their respects in the family cemetery, and he introduced them to his friends in Derzs.

The Greek Catholic priest studied the Hebrew primers Shumi sent him and acquainted the children with the language of the Old Testament. His ambition was to be able to read and translate the tombstones; he also wanted to make sure that the children to whom he taught religion understood something about Judaism and the Jews who had once lived in the village and helped it prosper.

By the early 1980s, weeding the Schwarcz cemetery had become a school project. In the mid-1980s, the children put flowers on the most recent Schwarcz graves on All Souls' Day, just as they did on their own family graves. When an adult told them that Jews don't observe All Souls' Day, the children wrote an anxious letter to Uncle Shumi: was it all right to observe a Christian custom in a Jewish cemetery?

The answer came by return mail: "I am grateful, and my ancestors were never so honored."

Having rejected the rituals of Judaism, Shumi crafted his own. For instance, he fasted once a year, from sunset to sunset, not on Yom Kippur, but on July 1, the day his family perished in Auschwitz.

He also devised what may be called the mixing of soils. When visiting the cemetery in Derzs, he scattered little bags of the gravelly, ash-laden gray soil he had collected in Auschwitz, where he had gone several times on pilgrimages, as well as bags of tawny sand he had brought from his two visits to the village of Sde Moshe in Israel, where his brothers Bédi and Anti had settled. He also placed, on his father's tombstone in Budapest, roses grown on the graves of his brother Mishi and sister Mara. He took fistfuls of sand from the Derzs cemetery to scatter in Auschwitz and over the family graves in Budapest.

Explaining his wish to be buried in Derzs, Shumi would tell his wife and other members of the family that he did not believe in afterlife or reincarnation and that he did not expect relatives to pray at his grave or even to visit it. "I am a rational man," Shumi said, and he defined his objective as the saving of the cemetery. If he succeeded in getting buried there, the cemetery wouldn't be liquidated for another thirty years. Who knows, he added, in years to come maybe someone else in the family will decide to be buried in Derzs, further extending the life of the cemetery.

As the years passed, Shumi's preparations for his return to Derzs became more and more detailed, and his insistence amounted to what even people other than his wife considered an obsession. "Our ancestors wrote lengthy wills distributing their wealth and asking their children to keep observing the Jewish law," said his nephew Levente, whom Shumi named his executor. "Uncle Shumi's last will and testament focused only on his burial."

Reluctantly, Shumi even made contact with officials of the collective farm in Derzs, who first looked upon him as someone who had stepped out of a museum: a courtly gentleman who used words they had heard only in the theater or read in books. Though they did not know what to say when he told them that he had been born in the building they used as their office, they soon saw that Shumi had no anger in him. He loved the land and the village the way one loves a a fiancee who died before the wedding. He even offered good advice on how to improve production; his examples were drawn from what he had learned in his visits to Israel. Using the colorful stories of a long lifetime as his only negotiating tools, he asked the local authorities to accept a special arrangement: to look the other way when he arrived on his last journey.

On May 29, 1988, Uncle Shumi died at the age of eighty-nine. He was buried just as he wished, next to his father and near his grandfather, after whom he was named. The school, the general store, and the entire collective farm closed down, while everyone from the village attended the funeral. The school children sang his favorite songs. His nephew Levente, who had arranged for the unplaned pine coffin, also brought a rabbi who performed a traditional service. A packet of soil from Jerusalem was placed under Shumi's head, just as it had been placed under the heads of his ancestors. As the coffin was lowered into the earth, the rabbi called out in a loud voice Shumi's Hebrew name, Shmuel, as a reminder to the soul because when judged in the other world, he will first be asked his name.

For the first time in more than forty years, a Jew was buried in the village of Derzs. For the first time in history, six Greek Catholic children read the Kaddish, the Hebrew prayer for the dead, which Shumi had typed up in Hungarian letters, all capitals for easier reading, and which he had asked to have them read aloud after his coffin was covered with dirt. The lead reader was a freckle-faced, talkative, cheerful little girl by the name of Kati. Kati Domokos.

Late spring is the time for locust trees to bloom, and no one was surprised that on the day of Shumi's funeral, the trees were in their full glory. Their sweet perfume wafted over the cemetery. The villagers said that the slender, pendulous clusters of white blooms, quivering in the wind, were never before as numerous as on the day the last landowner returned home.

Shumi's funeral in 1988.

ABOUT THE AUTHOR

Charles Fenyvesi is a writer at *U.S. News & World Report*, and contributes a gardening column to *The Washington Post*. He lives with his wife and three children in Washington, D.C., and cultivates a farm in Maryland.